P]

MW01235065

Always relevant, Harvey gives original answers to important questions – questions which matter in our daily lives. I admit now that some of these answers ('Society is a system of individual relationships') struck me at first as obvious – and then I realized that most answers are obvious, once you've already read them.... Part memoir, part meditation, Whiskey Wisdom is what can only be called a manifesto ... one specifically aimed at misfits, malcontents, unorthodox thinkers, self-starters, school-leavers, hard-workers. Like a hyena writing poetry upon tombstones, it is a howling cry and call for anyone who would undertake the task to do this: think for yourself – and in so doing, make the unimaginable imaginable, the impossible possible, the unthinkable thinkable, the undrinkable drinkable.

– James Cole, Professor Emeritus in poetry, University of Wyoming

Ray Harvey is a special writer, whose work will do what fine fiction must: take you on a journey from which you return transformed and renewed, seeing this world differently because of the world he has created. It is always heartening to find a new storyteller, and we can only hope that there will be more stories to come.

– **Nicholas Christopher,** author of *Veronica* and *A Trip to the Stars*

WHISKEY WISDOM
THE ART OF BEING INTERESTING

R. A. HARVEY

PEARL BUTTON PRESS

PRINTED IN THE UNITED STATES OF AMERICA.

FOR INFORMATION, PLEASE CONTACT
PEARL BUTTON PRESS, 305 W MAGNOLIA STREET #162
FORT COLLINS CO 80521.

WHISKEY WISDOM:
THE ART OF BEING INTERESTING

CONTENTS

WHISKEY WISDOM

PREFACE

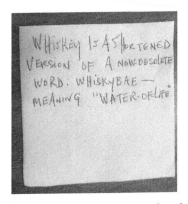

*Left on the bar by a fascinating guest whom I twice
had the pleasure of serving.*

Whiskey Wisdom represents a compendiation of certain nuggets of wisdom I've mined, over the course of two-plus decades, from the beautiful depths of the bar — a compendiation as well of the fascinating humans I've had the good fortune of serving and knowing over the course of those years:

from the freakishly clever, to the endlessly enlight-
ened, the breathtakingly levelheaded, the inexpress-
ibly kind, the spectacularly sweet, the immeasurably
generous, the wickedly cool, the wildly erudite, the
outrageously shrewd, the eye-poppingly practical,
the mind-spinningly articulate, the militantly non-
dogmatic, and everything in between.

I offer now these nuggets of wisdom to you.

An artist named David drew me shaking a martini.
I liked it so much that I had it framed.

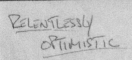

RELENTLESSLY
OPTIMISTIC

HER MOTHER AND FATHER
HAD NOT MEANT TO
NEGLECT HER.....

RELENTLESSLY OPTIMISTIC

HER MOTHER and father had never meant to neglect her. On the contrary, they'd always meant to love her — and they did love her — and yet Stephanie, the youngest of four, had come unexpectedly and somewhat late into their lives, and on top of that, she was sickly and accident-prone, susceptible to mishaps.

She was born with feet slightly malformed, and so she learned to crawl with corrective casts which went all the way up to her knees. When, at last, her casts came off, the child cried in horror, because in her child's mind these thick clunky appendages had become a part of her, and she missed them.

The summer she learned to walk, when arm-in-arm together her parents had unthinkingly swum away off the beach, and Stephanie had waddled after them into the ocean, she was nearly drowned — saved only by a swift and sharp-eyed passer-by, who, through the knifey sunlight, had spotted her floating facedown for what was nearly a lethal length of time.

Thin, anemic, asthmatic, she'd developed pneumonia five separate times before she was ten-years-old. The last two of those times, the doctors told her parents that she would probably not survive.

"She's grown too weak," the doctors said. "There's nothing more we can do. She's very undernourished, and at her young age, she's likely not strong enough to fight it."

But they were wrong.

And in spite of everything, she was the least complaining and the calmest of all their children. She never blamed, never sulked, never pouted. She was independent, solitary. Her eyesight was horrid, and yet she enjoyed reading. Often when she looked up from a book and smiled and her magnified eyes ignited behind those absurdly thick eye-glasses, the sight of this nearly brought her father to his knees: made him want to weep, futilely, with a complicated mixture of love and pity.

But Stephanie was not a person to be pitied, and she never thought of herself in this way. It wouldn't even have occurred to her. She was observant and contemplative, with an unbreakable glint in her near-sighted eyes, and her best feature was the radiant smile of innocence which so often broke open and bloomed across her face.

Growing up, she'd always had to fight to be heard. And fight she did.

On the snowy Christmas evening that our paths first crossed, when I was bartending at a Holiday Inn and she came into the lounge with a young man in a wheelchair (her son, I later learned), I overheard her say something to him as I served them their drinks, something that I think bears repeating now and always:

"Your ideas are your children, and they're all born handicapped," she said. "Just as each of us in our own way is also born handicapped. And everyone who wants his ideas to be heard has to fight for them."

IT'S NOT HOW CLEVER AND HOW SMART YOU ARE — IT'S HOW CLEVER AND SMART YOU WANT TO BE

THE MOST SUCCESSFUL people in life aren't particularly gifted or talented.

They become successful, rather, by wanting to be successful.

Genetic giftedness is largely a figment.

There are no such things as prodigies.

The emergent understanding of genetic expression has gone a long way in blasting to smithereens the entire notion of genetic predetermination.

Talent is a process.

Have you ever observed that the smartest kids in school are almost never the ones who go on to be the most successful in life?

School in its best state teaches datum, not ambition or desire or will — all of which things can be encouraged and fostered, but not really taught.

Ambition, desire, will, persistence — these, as

you may or may not guess, are the greatest predic-
tors of success.

———

No human being and no living thing begins her life
by undercutting it.

No human being, no matter how fortunate or
unfortunate, no matter how pampered, no matter
how abused, no matter how spoiled, no matter how
mistreated, starts out by giving up or giving in. No
one starts life irrevocably defeated.

Abandoning the dreams of one's youth comes
only after a protracted process of perversion.

The time it takes before this mindset dominates
differs for each person.

For most it is a gradual accretion of pressures
and setbacks and frustrations and small failures, or
by the systematic inculcation of mantras that this life
doesn't really matter, that our fellow humans have
rightful jurisdiction over our money and our time,
that our dreams can't be fully realized anyway, and
that human existence is accidental or meaningless or
both — only to one day discover that their passion,
once a glowing force within, is now gone … but
where and how?

Others, having no depth of thought or will, stop
at the first sign of adversity.

Only the truly passionate persist. Only the truly

passionate retain for a lifetime the vision they had of themselves when they were young. Only a handful maintain for a lifetime the beautiful vision of their youth and go on to give it form.

The means by which we give that vision form is our work.

No matter what any given person may become — no matter how good, bad, ugly, or great — in the April of life, each person at one time believes that her existence is important, and that big wonderful things await.

Each and every single human being has the potential to retain that vision, and each and every single human being *should* retain that vision, because it is the true and correct vision.

College, I submit, can do irreversible damage to it.

———

UNACTUALIZED POTENTIAL IS A TRAGEDY.

Nonconformity for nonconformity sake is meaningless.

Nonconformity for the sake of reason and independent thought, however, is a virtue.

Independent thought is a prerequisite of genius, and it takes courage to think for yourself.

Courage is also a virtue.

Blind conformity is the opposite of independent thought.

Ambition, too, is a virtue.

Virtue is human excellence. It is The Good.

The Good is that which fosters human life and promotes it.

The Bad, corollarily, is that which frustrates human life and smothers it. It is pain. It is that which stultifies human thought and human flourishing and prevents gain.

Thinking is the human method of living and prospering. It is for this reason that humans are properly defined as the rational animal, and it is for this same reason also that morality — true morality — is rooted not in God or gods or devils, but in the human quiddity: our conceptual apparatus, our rational faculty.

As a thing is defined by its identity, so humans are defined by their acts — which is to say, their actions.

Our actions are in turn shaped by our thoughts.

Your brain is without question the most powerful weapon in your arsenal. And nothing increases its strength like thinking. Cultivate, therefore, deliberate thought.

It is the greatest asset you've got.

YOUR LIFE IS LARGELY a process of turning your interests into talents, which is done through a process of practice.

Talent is learned. It is cultivated.

Talent is not fated.

Your talents are rooted in the things you most enjoy doing.

It is in this sense that your passions are primarily willed.

Find your passions and grow them, and the more you do this, the more completely you'll be fulfilled.

IF YOU WANT to go to college, go.

If your true desire requires something specialized or technical — like medicine or engineering or law — go.

By all means, this.

The point here is not to condemn college categorically, for condemnation sake.

The point here — the only point here — is that if you're going to college because that's what you've been told you should do, or because you've been told that you must go to college in order to have a more complete or successful life, do not go.

Do not go to college merely for lack of anything better.

If you don't yet know what you want to do, do not go.

Don't go back to college for that Bachelor's degree in sociology.

Don't go back to college to try and motivate yourself to write, or in an attempt to fill your time or your head.

Cultivate your brain instead.

Read. Think. Blink. Drink.

Relax.

Be self-taught.

Learn to play the piano or piccolo or sax.

Read and think a lot.

There is no hurry — I assure you, there is no hurry.

I assure you, you need not worry. In fact, in a great many ways, it is a good thing to not yet know what you want, because life is a gigantic canvas and there's so much with which to fill it, so much to do — haven't you heard? So much, indeed, that choosing one thing at twenty or thirty or even forty is absurd.

College is far from the be-all-and-the-end-all. College is a lot of conformity and groupthink. It can truly stunt your brain, every bit as much as lack of nourishment or food.

College is very often nothing more than pointless debt accrued.

———

YOUR DESIRE TO become the person you most want to become is ultimately the only thing you need.

In its elaboration, this will require a great deal — focus, discipline, practice, more practice — but the desire is the fundamental thing.

As long as there's a fundamental desire and it burns like a ball of gasoline-and-fire, there's no boundary to anyone's achievement — none whatsoever. You needn't be a so-called savant.

The desire to soar is the most important factor in becoming what you want.

———

"LIFE IS an unceasing sequence of single actions, but the single action is by no means isolated," wrote Ludwig von Mises.

Your life is largely a process of transforming your interests into talents, which, in turn, comes about through a process of practice. It is in this sense, I say again, that your passions are primarily willed, and not inborn or innate.

Even genius is willed.

You make yourself great.

———

MOZART WAS NOT A PRODIGY. He was a workhorse. *Aussi* the Polgar sisters, and all the rest.

Life is work.

Jobs are healthy.

Work is good.

Work is good for the soul.

Be happy in your work.

Nothing more fundamental than labor is required for the production of abundance and the good things that you want for your life.

Labor takes many forms.

Blue-collar jobs build character, as they build invaluable work habits that you'll never lose.

In her book *No Shame in My Game,* Katherine Newman, to her great credit, explicitly points out what for many of us has been implicitly obvious from as far back as we can remember: namely, that so-called low-skilled, blue-collar jobs, whether fast-food, waitressing, bartending, barista, custodial, clerking, so on, they require talents completely commensurate with, or even surpassing, white-collar work:

"Memory skills, inventory management, the ability to work with a diverse crowd of employees, and versatility in covering for co-workers when the demand increases," she writes — and I would add: many, many other skills, as well.

Servers, bartenders, baristas, expos, clerks, et cetera, must multitask and remember every bit as much as, for example, an ER doc — as more than one ER doc, seated in front of me at my work, has specifically said.

This is one of the many reasons these jobs are good, and not something anybody should knock — and anybody who does knock them is an elitist fool, destined to become a cipher of history.

On that, you may quote me wildly.

WHAT DO YOU VALUE? What things do you love the most? The active work of your body and brain?

Find work that you enjoy and embrace it. Become good at it. Become better. Pour your energy into your work like rain. Enjoy the motions of your body in concert with your brain.

She who's faithful in a little is faithful in a lot.

Everything you do, therefore, do it with all that you've got.

HOW TO BE WICKEDLY
CHARISMATIC

THE ART of charisma is the art of personality, and personality is personal style. It is individuality.

Which is why there are as many different ways to be charismatic as there are different styles of personality.

Personality is the sum total of one's many individual characteristics as they come together and create the person presented to the world.

Just as a thing is defined by its identity, so humans are defined by their acts, which are in turn defined by their thoughts.

Since we're each the shapers of our own thoughts — and *only* our own thoughts — we each have the power to shape and mold our own personality.

For this reason, charisma begins (and ends) in the brain.

Charisma is magnetism.

Magnetism, as the very word implies, is the power to attract.

People can be magnetic and charismatic in a multitude of different ways:

You don't, for instance, need to be extroverted to be charismatic. You don't need to be gregarious or boisterous. Many of the most charismatic people you've ever seen are silent and strange.

Nor is physical beauty alone charismatic — or, at any rate, not in the full sense of the word:

Physical beauty attracts, visually, esthetically, sexually, whathaveyou, but its power of attraction is limited — limited precisely because humans are sapient creatures, which means we think and ruminate and interact.

Magnetic qualities are ultimately qualities that demonstrate one's skills at living life as humans are made to live it — which is to say, cognitively. This is why contemplation is among the highest occupations of the human species.

Personality and behavior are a complex interplay of contemplation and action mixed. But it all originates in the brain. Which, in general terms, is the reason that the most magnetic quality anyone can possess is the authentic happiness and the relaxed disposition that comes from a life that's been well-considered and thus well-lived. A healthy sense of self is a natural reflection of that.

Perfection, however — and this is important — is

not the determining factor in matters magnetic and charismatic:

Flaws, faults, foibles, and fuck-ups do not an uncharismatic person make.

How one *deals* with one's own flaws, faults, foibles, and fuck-ups is what's at primary issue.

Happiness is charismatic.

Understanding is charismatic.

Authentic self-confidence is charismatic because it discloses efficacy and self-worth.

Have you ever observed that you're at your best when you're doing something you genuinely grasp?

Have you ever observed that you're at your most relaxed and comfortable when you're doing something you enjoy — i.e. something that you're genuinely confident in?

That state of mind is charismatic.

Have you, on the other hand, noticed that when you're put into a situation about which you know little or nothing and want no real part of, you feel diffident, timid, not very happy?

This is the opposite of charismatic.

"Reason is a faculty for the integration of knowledge that human beings possess," wrote Spinoza, and with him here I do not demur. The primary method of human survival is found precisely in our faculty of reason, because of which human survival isn't just physical but psychological.

This is why happiness is the ends but *not* the

means: the goal of life is emotional, but the means of achieving it are not emotional. The means of achieving it are cognitive, epistemological:

We must use our brains.

We must think.

Charisma stems from this uniquely human faculty. Charisma comes from the mind.

"The highest activity a human being can attain is learning for understanding sake, because to understand is to be free," Spinoza also said.

Cultivate, I repeat, your powers of thought — cultivate contemplation — and in the very decision to do this, your charisma like a soft ripple-effect will grow and grow.

THE AWESOME POWER OF
YOUR EYES

HUMAN EYES ARE ELECTRIC, the gaze of each person charged with live-wire voltage — capable of searing permanent impressions into any new acquaintance's brain. The awesome power of your eyes is magnified, moreover, the moment you lock onto another's gaze — the power of the human stare drastically intensified the instant two humans fasten eyes upon each other.

One evening when I was giving an uninspired talk that I'd not signed-up for, the subject-matter of which was the murky origins of the martini, I suddenly glimpsed across the room, in a crowd of about fifty, a bright and beaming face, which shone from deep among the shadows. It was a face that at once leapt out at me, energizing me, so that for the rest of my talk, this face was my primary focal point. It wasn't a particularly striking or otherwise noteworthy face, and yet I instantly fixed my focus upon it because this man, a shy and quiet gent with whom I'd two or three times crossed paths, never once while I spoke broke eye contact with me. In fact, he watched me in a way that made it sincerely seem as though he was hanging upon my every word, sometimes even cocking his head and narrowing his eyes in a look of real curiosity. His attentiveness and his concentration galvanized me, encouraged me to share my knowledge (such as it was) and made me want to deliver the story in richer and more powerful terms — and this, I'm here to tell you, is a perfect illustration of the awesome power contained inside your eyes.

"The eye is so constituted that one can perceive the soul that flows beneath it," wrote Victor Hugo, and he is unquestionably correct. The reason this is so is that the human mind has at its disposal the power of comprehension, which is no small thing, and the eyes, in turn, are twins wells that open to our comprehending minds.

"We assert ourselves by the light that lies underneath our eyelids," Victor Hugo continued. "Small consciousnesses shift and dart and blink their eyes. Large souls cast down thunderbolts with their gaze."

Strong eye contact signals intelligence — there is no doubt about this — suggesting, as it does, an abstract thinker who can at the same time listen and also easily process new information in a steady stream as the information flows in. (Some psychologists have even theorized that this is why intelligent people seem more comfortable maintaining eye contact during silences: because intelligent people are actively thinking, occupying their minds.)

Everyone knows also that good eye contact is magnetic, whereas poor eye contact is a sign of diffidence or distraction or both. Shifty eyes are fidgety eyes, and fidgety eyes do not attract but repel. And they repel because they indicate that the shifty-eyed soul isn't listening.

Listening is always magnetic.

Be slow to speak and swift to hear, and your eyes will reveal your patience which you contain within you. Before you speak, pause a beat or two and then begin, and your eyes will show a person comfortable enough to allow this sort of sedate silence. Slower speakers are universally regarded as more engaging than those who speak rapidly — in part because speaking slowly discloses a soul that considers things before speaking: a soul that ponders, perpends. Speak, therefore, more carefully, and speak also at the appropriate volume for the room or place you're in, and your eyes will match your mien.

"Volume and how appropriate it is for your circumstances shows a strong sense of self," says psychologist Wendell Barry.

Good eye contact, however, means *relaxed* eye

contact. Good eye contact is not, in other words, some fierce, hyper-unwavering stare.

If you have trouble holding somebody's eyes, try actively observing the multitude of different colors contained within those eyes. Make a scientific study of the shades and colors, and pay attention to them. This will shift your focus away from the task of maintaining eye contact, making you less self-conscious thereby.

Or count the person's blinks, which has been demonstrated by cognitive psychologists as an effective method for maintaining proper eye contact.

Or look at the eyelashes. Notice the individual strands and count them if you can.

A most memorable bar guest I served on and off for one full summer — a lean and wiry seventy-year-old fellow, whose toffee-colored skin was like elephant hide, a man who went by the name of Vasco even though his real name was Kenneth, and who, though born in Wyoming and back for a three-month visit, lived on a remote Caribbean island — once told me his method for maintaining perfect eye contact:

"Look only at the tip of the nose," said Vasco. "And she'll never know that you're not looking directly into her eyes."

He was right.

Try this experiment:

Look at yourself in your phone-camera, or your

bathroom mirror. Then close your eyes and think of something that's made you feel unequivocally, irre-pressibly happy — happy to be alive. Concentrate on that thing. Actually put yourself back in the moment, so that you're feeling the happiness all over again, and make yourself feel it for at least a half-minute.

Now open your eyes and observe what your eyes look like in that precise instant.

That's what magnetic eye contact looks like: relaxed and soft and happy.

HOW TO PENETRATE PEOPLE'S
BRAINS AS THOUGH YOU'RE
TELEPATHIC

THE HUMAN FACE is capable of over five thousand different expressions and micro-expressions, and every one of these reveals some facet of your private thoughts. Every movement of your body, every stance, every position, every pose — the multitude of different ways in which you *move* — this is your soul in motion: the most accurately written autobiography that could ever be authored.

No one, of course, is *actually* telepathic, because telepathy doesn't exist, but by paying close attention to the ways in which people move and to the expressions and micro-expression people make, you can learn to read people as *though* you're telepathic.

Once, not so very long ago, when I was bartending alone on a Monday afternoon at a little jazz lounge called Ace Gillett's, a man came in by himself and sat down at a small table near the entrance. I'd just opened up for the day, and so no one except the two of us was there. I poured this guest a glass of water chocked full of ice and then came around the bar to serve him at his table. The moment before I set his ice-water in front of him, I saw him ever-so-slightly yet unmistakably double-take the glass in my hand. He said nothing, however, and yet I knew in an instant — or, at any rate, I strongly suspected.

"No ice in your water," said I.

"Yes," he said. "How did you know?"

"It's like I read your mind."

In actuality, of course, his double-take (of which he likely had no conscious awareness) was what tipped me off, and this guest — this guest in particular, as I was shortly to learn — quickly deduced that it was something like this.

"Oh, that was good," he said.

This little exchange then prompted a deeper and more fascinating conversation.

As it turned out, this man was a neurologist — had gone from ER doc back to medical school to specialize in neurology — and he and I soon became friends. On that initial visit, after I'd dumped out his ice-water and then poured and served him a fresh glass with no ice, he told me about a class he'd once taken on non-verbal tells and the science of body language. He was a serious poker player, he said, who often competed in tournaments, where the stakes were high, and this class he'd taken had come highly recommended by a fellow poker player. The class was taught by a retired FBI agent, who for thirty-five years had specialized in this very subject: profiling suspects by means of their body language and facial expressions.

"It was a two-day class," the neurologist told me, "and I paid a thousand dollars for it, and I did so to better hone my poker skills. It was worth every cent."

He then said that while the class did indeed benefit his poker game ("inestimably," as he put it), it was what it did for his medical practice that truly changed his outlook: specifically, he said, in how it taught him to read patients more accurately than ever before.

He said that learning to observe and interpret non-verbal behavior altered his entire perspective and his medical work — altered it in ways he'd never have anticipated: the movements and fidgets and facial expressions of his patients often saying the exact opposite of what their words said.

Why is this so?

It's so because non-verbal behavior is subconscious and automatic, and if a person doesn't know she or he is being observed, it's near-infallible. It is everywhere, and it is often more reliable than words.

Once you learn even a small portion of what's communicated by means of face-and-body language, you'll be astonished — astonished at the things you're able to decode just by observing the movements and micro-movements of everyone with whom you come in contact.

I assure you, this is no pseudo-science or quackery, and, in fact, the whole pseudo-science of so-called psychics relies in large measure upon this very thing.

Do you doubt it?

I ask you to consider what I wrote in the first paragraph of this chapter: the human face alone is capable of over five thousand expressions and micro-expressions, and the human body apart from the face is capable of many more on top of that.

Now ask yourself: are *any* of these movements and gestures and expressions telling?

Pursed lips?

A frown?

A wince?

A crooked smile?

Raised eyebrows?

Crossed arms?

Rubbing the back of the neck?

Open palms?

A crinkled nose?

A nostril flare?

A step backward?

Downcast eyes?

Shifty eyes?

Shifting from foot-to-foot?

A turn to the left, away from you?

A turn to the right, closer to you?

Clenched fists?

You see: even the most untrained person can decode the more obvious non-verbals.

If you're still skeptical, try this:

Pull up a video clip of a movie or a television show you've never seen before and mute the volume.

Pay attention to what you're watching with no sound.

I guarantee you that if you pay attention, you'll understand a great deal of what's going on merely from the movements and micro-movements of the actors. This is true even if it's a scene with only two people talking.

The brain, understand, is ultimately what drives all human behavior — whether that behavior is conscious or subconscious — and our body language comes from a vast complexity of factors, entirely individualized, which, like a barometer, registers our automatic emotional responses. This fact, which may sound obvious and even simplistic but which in actuality is a principle of the profoundest sort, is the thing that gives rise to the silent language of human faces and human bodies. It is this principle which forms the underpinnings of all non-verbal behavior.

Watch people when they aren't aware that they're being watched and do you know what you'll see?

You'll see a gallery of emotional activity.

Glance secretly, for example, at the face of your dinner guest while she's eating the meal you prepared — if, that is, you want to know how she *actually* feels about your food. Or the face of your partner beside you while you're driving to visit your parents. Or the bar guest reading messages on his phone.

In a very real sense, as the neurologist said to me the afternoon we first met, body language often conveys more significant information than words, because at any stage beyond early childhood, body language is a subconscious response — an immediate reaction that comes from factors once consciously programmed. Traumatic experiences, to take an extreme example, can create all sorts of non-verbal reactions, which after the trauma, often become fully automated, subconscious responses *to* the trauma, and it takes a great deal of conscious effort and practice to reprogram such reactions — whereas words, which are consciously chosen, can easily be changed and manipulated. If, for instance, you're a doctor trying to diagnose a certain condition in a woman who's come to see you, and you ask her if she's been using any street drugs, this woman can easily and instantaneously say no — out of embarrassment, self-consciousness, fear of legal ramifications, whathaveyou. But watch the immediate reaction of her eyes, or the slight brief nod of her head, or if either of her hands become restless, and you may well get a more accurate answer.

Consider also that no matter how powerful your verbal message, if your body language is wrong, you'll not have the presence you want your words to convey.

If, on the other hand, your body language is right, this alone will divulge much about you, apart from your verbal message.

"In the last 20 years, we've learned more about the communicative power of the human face than in the previous 20 millennia," wrote Daniel McNeill in his excellent book *The Face: A Natural History*. And, I would add, in the meaning of body movements and micro-movements as well, which, in collaboration with the face, tells the world the true tale of the human soul.

HOW TO CHARM THE PANTS OFF ANYONE WITHOUT SAYING A SINGLE WORD

THE FOLLOWING ARE five silent ways to charm the pants off anyone.

SMILE SINCERELY but esoterically

There are many different types of smiles.

There are fake smiles and there are cold smiles.

There are warm smiles and there are sly smiles.

There are guilty smiles and there are devilish smiles.

The principle that really matters is to smile sincerely but not too quickly.

Unquestionably, a large warm smile is *always* uplifting and inviting and good, and you'll never go wrong with it.

A large warm smile that's slightly delayed, however — that's even better.

Why?

Because it inundates people with a sudden gush of happiness that's meant exclusively for them.

Don't slouch

Stand up tall, lift your chin a little, and show the world your joy at the mere fact of being alive.

"Good posture and a purposeful walk — shoulders lifted, though not in an exaggerated or uncomfortable manner, back straight, not overbearing but comfortable in how you stand and face the world — these are also signs of a healthy sense of self," says psychologist Wendell Barry.

Hold their eyes

Hold their eyes, yes, but hold them *softly.*

This is more important than you may realize. Maintain eye contact, as previously mentioned, but don't do it with a ferocious and fevered gaze.

Make your eye contact gentle and kind. And remember: if at first you have trouble keeping eye contact, look instead at the tip of their nose, or, better yet, count their blinks, or scrutinize the multitudinous colors within their eyes.

When, at last, you look away, look away *slowly.*

. . .

FACE the person

People won't generally like you until they know you like them. This a truism, but it's one that holds up well.

Turn, therefore, fully toward a person and show the person by your stance that you are open and friendly — a friendly presence.

This in collaboration with your slow flooding smile will put people instantly at ease by showcasing your likable disposition.

DON'T FIDGET

As you don't fidget with your eyes, so also don't fidget with your body.

Repose is always magnetic because repose is a hallmark of a relaxed disposition, which originates in the mind, and this, in turn, confers a sense of calm. Calm is contagious.

Thus: don't paw at your face.

Don't wiggle your fingers.

Don't open and close your fists.

Don't shift from foot to foot.

Don't nod too frequently.

Be *still*.

Be tranquillo.

Tranquillo Cocktail

2 ounces Mezcal

1 ounce Absinthe

.5 ounces Cointreau

.5 ounces Fresh Lemon Juice

.5 ounces Fresh Lime Juice.

Shake Vigorously & Serve up.

HOW TO HAVE PEOPLE DYING TO
HEAR WHAT YOU'LL SAY NEXT

DON'T SPEAK.

Just listen.

Listen well.

Listen attentively.

Be the silent one.

Be the listener while everyone else is doing the talking.

Finally, after everyone else has talked and talked, say something at last.

I guarantee you — I absolutely *guarantee* you — that every single person will be dying to hear what you have to say.

HOW TO ANSWER THE AGE-OLD
QUESTION: WHAT DO YOU DO?

"I RIDE motorcycles and make love to beautiful women," said the cool guy who worked on an assembly line in a glass factory — who adored women and who rode his motorcycle every chance he got. He was sitting at the bar answering a lovely lady who'd just asked him the age-old question.

His answer, I thought, was a very good answer. The lovely lady thought so as well.

If, however, you're not in the mood to respond quite so obliquely or provocatively, may I suggest that at the bare minimum, you always do this:

Give enough information about what you do that people can work with it. This is true, incidentally, no matter what your occupation.

If you're a waitress, for instance, perhaps say something like this:

"I'm a waitress. Do you eat french fries? If you do,

the diner where I work serves french fries *so* good, they'll haunt you till they're gone."

If you're a computer programmer, maybe say something like:

"I write computer programs. I speak the language of code. It is a heavy load. Code is poetry. Do you speak it? It's okay if you don't. I speak semi-fluent English as well, and so we'll most likely still be able to communicate."

If you're a garbage-hauler, you can say what I once heard an actual garbage-hauler say:

"I'd tell you, but you'd think it was total garbage. Okay. I'm a trash-hauler. It's an honest dollar."

The idea, whether you like my examples or not, is that no matter what you do — from the bluest of blue-collar jobs to the whitest of white-collar jobs — give your interlocutor something into which she can sink her teeth and *chew,* so that she then might more easily regurgitate something back at you.

Perhaps most important of all, never forget what Edgar Watson Howe once wrote:

"No man would listen to you talk if he didn't know it was his turn next."

HOW TO BECOME A FREAKISHLY BRILLIANT SMALL-TALKER BY DOING ONE SIMPLE THING

What is the one simple thing?

It is this:

Make people feel relaxed.

Small talk is not primarily about content. It's about commiseration.

When you ask someone for the time and you're told how to build a clock, you'll not easily move forward in the conversation.

When, upon the other hand, you ask for the time, and you're told "I don't know: the battery in my phone died, and it is a sad pass indeed when a grown man can't tell the time without his smart-phone, don't you agree?" — you will likely be put more at ease.

Think of conversation as a kind of stroll. Think of it as a stroll that may or may not progress, depending upon your first few steps. Think of small talk as those first steps — and remember that those steps consist only of one or two sentences.

The secret is to get in synch — to match stride — with whomever you're talking to.

Small talk, I say again, isn't primarily about content. It's about commiseration.

It's about mood.

Make whomever you're speaking to feel comfortable, and you're more than halfway there.

HOW TO COME ACROSS AS
DIABOLICALLY CLEVER

"IF YOU WANT to come across as diabolically clever," said the lady English professor, apropos of something I'd just missed on the television set above my head (this at the first bar I ever worked, in my salad days, when I was green in judgment and hot in blood), "all the degrees and all the accolades in the world pale in comparison to one thing."

"What is it?" I asked. "What is the one thing?"

"Learn to use *who* and *whom* correctly."

This, she continued (and I admit I was already putty in this pretty lady's hands), will signal cleverness more than any other single thing.

Was she correct? I really don't know — but I do know this: it can't hurt.

I know also that if a good-looking English professor for whom you just made a Maker's Mark Mint Julep — triple strong — deems the correct use of *who* and *whom* as "diabolically clever," you at twenty-one years of age, in your salad days, green in judgment and hot in blood, are going to by-God do your level best to keep those two words straight forevermore.

I know also that you'll never go wrong if you only use *who* and avoid *whom* altogether. In fact, some grammarians believe that *whom* is slowly dying off, a natural death, and will one day soon be an extinct lexical species.

One thing for sure: nothing makes you sound less clever than misusing the word *whom* — and here's an actual example of what I mean:

"Our server," somebody once emailed me, in a letter of complaint when I was managing-and-bartending at a beautiful little jazz lounge called Ace Gillett's, "whom never gave us her name ..."

Now I ask in all sincerity: How will you ever take *that* letter seriously?

———

BECAUSE YOUR WORDS are your thoughts concretized, it is in large measure your words that make you clever — and please take note of that phrasing: your words don't merely make you *appear* clever. They *make* you clever: because humans think by means of words, and so without language, there is no thought.

Cultivate wordplay, therefore. Seek to describe things in a colorful and unorthodox manner:

"Hey, bartender, what's that mint-green bottle that stands out so clearly among the multicolored glass?"

You see?

That's good language. It's also an actual thing a guest once said to me.

"It's TYKU," I replied, without so much as a glance behind me — so felicitous his phrasing, so perfect his description. "A citrus saki."

———

BE PERSUASIVE. How? Learn facts and remember them. Speak clearly and concisely and avoid jargon. This, without any doubt, is among the most persuasive and universal signs of cleverness there is:

Because the more clearly and concisely you're able to articulate something, the more clearly you grasp it yourself.

And those who speak well speak briefly.

———

CULTIVATE YOUR MEMORY. There is really no such thing as a poor memory: there is only the untrained memory — and memory likes to be trusted.

When you trust your memory, you train your memory.

Strive to remember quips, quotes, anecdotes. Develop a deeper well from which to draw — rather than recycling the same three or four or five, like me: the ol' broken record. It always delights a person when she or he hears a new story from an old friend.

Most important of all — at all costs, I mean, and by all means available, even if you have to move heaven and earth to do it — avoid stale cliches like the plague. Even thinking about it has me sweating like a pig. I mean, my heart is really beating like a drum.

Yet certain cliches, if they've been gone from the vernacular long enough, are colorful and charming — you have to exercise your judgement here, and I don't pretend it's an exact science:

"Sharks?" she said to me. "Swimming with them? Well that's a different kettle of fish entirely, cowboy."

Oh, I was putty in her hands alright.

NEVER — and I mean *never* — make a joke at someone else's expense for the sake of a laugh.

"Hey, baldie! Can you turn your head? The glare coming off you is blinding me."

It's tacky, it's amateurish, and, worst of all, it's fiercely unfunny.

DON'T ASK the age-old question: "What do you do?"

Instead, say something like this:

"What in life brings you bliss?"

("God," she answered. "I spend virtually all my waking hours at work, and so I'm afraid there's little time for bliss." At which point, almost magically, many conversational options have suddenly opened up before you, among which is the fact that you are now — only now — at liberty to ask what it is that occupies her time so.)

DON'T USE big or biggish words which you only partially understand — no matter how brobdingnagian your brain and no matter your predilection for sesquipedalianism. (Sorry.) But *do* cultivate a bigger vocabulary.

This is easier than you might think. Begin by learning a new word every few days and then incorporate that word into your writing or your speech. Also, learn fresher, less common words for standard things. Instead of saying, for instance, "You look beautiful tonight," try:

"You look particularly radiant this evening."

Which, incidentally, I once heard a very kind and clever fellow say to a middle-age woman he knew, though only a little, who had just sat down next to him at the bar, and this woman, who *did* look particularly radiant that night, was, I swear to you, walking on sunshine all evening long from this one compliment alone.

In fact, I took special note of that — in large part because it so clearly and so significantly lifted her, and she was such a sweet though slightly sad soul, who had lost her husband to suicide. I even wrote this exchange down on a napkin I no longer have. And I wrote it because I found it very touching.

TEN AUTHENTIC SIGNS OF INTELLIGENCE THAT CANNOT BE FAKED

INTELLIGENCE IS your brain's capacity to deal with a wide range of thoughts and ideas.

Like most things, therefore, intelligence is a *process.*

It is not a static state.

It is not something you either do or don't at birth possess.

Your brain is something you cultivate.

Intelligence stems fundamentally from thinking.

Thinking is a choice. It requires one essential thing: effort.

Thought is work. Thought is effort.

Thinking develops your brain. It increases your intellectual power and range.

Non-thought, corollarily, is something you can change.

You *become* brilliant.

You *learn* to be smart.

You are not afraid of new ideas because you know your brain can measure and weigh and test these new ideas — in the same way your brain can create new onomatopoeias.

A cultivated mind is an intelligent mind.

It is also beautiful and strange and rather difficult to find.

Thought is both the source and also the end result: it is the goal. It is the driving force.

Intelligence is your ability to think.

This ability can be habituated and developed, or not, depending chiefly upon what you most prefer to do with your time.

You know you're in the presence of a brain that's been intelligently cultivated when you see some of the following:

Fast, fluid handwriting that's legible

There's a misbegotten notion that illegibility is a sign of a smart person, when in actuality it's the other way around:

People who write legibly want to be understood. Thus they make an effort to present themselves clearly, which takes brain power. Quick clear handwriting shows practice and patience, which in turn shows cognitive cultivation.

Which is not to say that the opposite necessarily indicates unintelligence — it doesn't necessarily — though it does often indicate a certain lack of concern for the delicate art of explication.

A CLEVER WIT invariably signals that someone's mind has been cultivated

Wit is mental sharpness. It is cognitive acuity. It is cleverness. It is keenness.

Similarly — and for the same reasons — people who like to laugh, and who in turn like to make others laugh, are to that extent unfailingly intelligent.

The word "wit," incidentally, is the root of the word "wisdom," which is in turn a derivative of the Proto-Germanic *witz*, the Old Saxon *witt*, in Old Norse *vit*, in Danish *vid*, in Swedish *vett*, Old High German *wizzi* — all of which may be translated as "mental capacity, knowledge, understanding; to know."

A sharp sense of time and direction show brain power

Why?

Because a sharp sense of time and direction indicate attention and focus.

The choice to focus or not is the seat of human thought.

The choice to pay attention is where it begins — and ends. It is the locus.

SMART PEOPLE by definition are more curious

They are thus more tolerant of ambiguity, just as they are also more tolerant of differences in others — grasping, as they do, what for many is obvious:

The brain is a complicated place, and largely for this reason no two people are alike. This basic act of apprehension gives any person who performs it a more complex and sophisticated mode of thinking.

All humans by their nature desire to know, as Aristotle said. This fundamental fact is the very seat of curiosity, which, in turn, provokes investigation, study, learning.

OBSESSIVE WORRY IS an indicator of intelligence, because it discloses a racing mind that's never at rest but always thinking, always considering

Which is why some of the greatest thinkers and innovators in world history were and are monomaniacal ruminators.

SMART PEOPLE LIKE to read for fun

People who take active pleasure in reading, rather than doing so out of duty and rather than reading purely for information, without any real joy or enthusiasm in the act, unquestionably have brains they've worked to cultivate — which means, among other things (and studies do confirm): avid readers have better memory function, communication skills, and focus.

TRULY INTELLIGENT PEOPLE like to often be alone

Which doesn't necessarily mean they're introverted (although they can be), nor does it mean they don't like spending time among friends and with other people.

Rather, intelligent people prefer much privacy and space, just as they prefer to pick and choose the time they spend among others, precisely because they are more independent, and they value their independence — in part, perhaps, because it gives them time to think, as well as time to relax. Smart people — genuinely smart people, as against the book-smart and the pedantic and all the other imposters — are autonomous, and as such they have the authentic confidence that can only come from thought and the comprehension that thinking fosters.

INTELLIGENT PEOPLE ARE self-aware

They know themselves. And because they know

themselves, intelligent people recognize their mistakes and failures, and strive to learn from them.

Self-awareness and insight into self is one of the few infallible signs of intelligence.

PEOPLE WHO CAN ARGUE ARTICULATELY and convincingly — and from many different angles — have, to that extent, clearly cultivated their brains

Their minds through practice are able to move nimbly from one idea to another, like a long-legged water-spider skating across the surface of a river.

YET THEY ARE OFTEN slow to speak and swift to hear

Genuinely smart people make a habit of thinking about what they're going to say before they say it. Their brains, also through practice, are honed in such a way that their brain has become quicker than their mouth.

WHAT, after all, does it mean to be smart?

It means to stylize your mind, like a work of art.

It means to cultivate your thoughts for as long as you're alive — cultivate your thoughts as if they're the plants of a living garden.

Cultivate them, yes, before your ideas, only

partially thought through, ooze into dogma and then fully harden.

It means to observe the universe around you, as well as the one within: to introspect, as thoughtful people do.

It means to be intelligent, like you.

LYNCHPIN

FOR YOU, the secret was never a secret, quite, because for you it always seemed natural — not necessarily easy, of course, but obvious, and obviously right.

It never mystified you, perhaps because you learned long ago that your body is a ship, your brain the pilot at the tip.

Which is why everything you ever decided to do you learned to do with skill, having discovered that in matters such as these the decisive factor is the human will.

You discovered that the secret key to the lock of life is nothing more — or less — than developing a durable purpose around which to arrange all the other things in your life, and against which all other things are measured and weighed.

This, in any case, is what you conveyed.

A central purpose, as you say, is the unifying factor that molds together the human clay and integrates all the other factors in your life, year-to-year, month-to-month, day-to-day. So that to be in control of your own life, you must *develop* this fundamental purpose, and then not let it go.

But why? Why is this so?

Because purpose forms the base and at the same time creates a kind of pyramid, the subsequent stones of which are your other desires, arranged in order of importance. This, in turn, spares you any number of internal clashes and strife. This great pyramid is your life.

The central purpose that forms its base allows you to enjoy existence more abundantly, and on the widest conceivable scale.

You, having discovered this long ago, could never after that truly go too far astray, or too disastrously fail.

All the rest fell naturally into place.

It's one reason people argue about the liveliness of your eyes. It's why they discuss the ineffable quality of your face.

She was always a little reckless, they say, a reckless shooter, a long-shot, a shoot-from-the-hipper, but despite her wild misses always, deep down, believed she could be a star. There's a certain languorous confidence about her (they say) a certain laid-back quality that's fascinating, yes, but somehow it seems taken a little far.

It makes her remote and solitary, like a star.

Still, she's kind and well-spoken and oddly charismatic, if rather fanatic, who never cared to hunt with the horde — indeed, never hunted at all — but chose instead to focus first upon the work, whatever it was (night-audit, waitress, secretary, clerk), not the parties or the party boys or the alcohol-fueled life.

Nor, indeed, was there ever the all-consuming passion to be somebody's girlfriend, or mistress, or wife.

Work is healthy, you say, jobs are good for the soul. Work provides an outlet for creativity and expression. Life is work. Life is purposeful effort. It is an unceasing sequence of individual actions. Productive work is for this reason not meant to be a perfunctory performance, or jail sentence. It's just the opposite: it's a creative act, an act that's nourishing.

Productive effort is the *sine-qua-non* of human happiness and flourishing.

It's your continual progress forward, one step to another, one step at a time, one achievement to another, always upward and always guided by the continual growth of your mind, your knowledge, your inexhaustible versatility and limitless ingenuity.

Be happy in your work.

Do you at any time reach a point when it's too late to find a purpose, ever?

No, you say, never.

ARE YOU FASCINATING?

WELL, are you, punk?

Or are you boring as hell?

How, furthermore, can you tell?

How can you tell if you're an inveterate bore, or if you're just in a kind of long-term funk?

Much of what we hear about commanding attention and the power to fascinate is theoretical and abstract, a sort of psychological jargon: fascination triggers, hotspots, personality tests and the like.

Let us, for once, get concrete.

Here, from a bartender's perspective, are seven differences between the fascinating person and the boring piece of meat:

. . .

FASCINATING PEOPLE HAVE **many activities they enjoy and become good at, which gives them a greater wealth of material to mine**

Boring people have one or perhaps two.

Diversify your activity portfolio, and through this one thing alone, you'll have come a long way in becoming irresistibly fascinating.

FASCINATING PEOPLE COMMUNICATE **what most others can't — or they communicate it in ways most others don't**

Words, contrary to popular belief, are not primarily for communicating — which is their secondary function. Their primary function is for clarity of thought.

Before one can communicate clearly, one must have something *to* communicate clearly.

Language brings about this process.

The desire for clarity presupposes the desire to be understood, and this is why the ability to communicate clearly — in writing or in speech — is one of the surest signs of intelligence there is.

And intelligence, as you know, is always fascinating.

FASCINATING PEOPLE AREN'T **afraid to try new things — which means**

They're not only willing to break out of their comfort zone but also motivated to do so. Why?

Because they know that comfort breeds complacency.

Interesting people, understand, are, to one degree or another, adventurous. They like to get out and explore.

Because life is largely an adventure — provided it's treat as such.

FASCINATING PEOPLE ARE *au courant*

They keep up-to-date on at least some news.

Which is why as a bartender you often find yourself charmed by those customers who have a certain knowledge of music or current books and current movies and other pop-culture things: because this, too, shows that an effort is being made to stay informed.

Thus:

FASCINATING PEOPLE ARE knowledgable

Boring people are poorly informed — and so they're often unable to hold up their end of a conversation.

Being poorly informed, let it be noted, is entirely within each person's control.

The better informed you are, the more you'll have to talk about.

The more you have to talk about, the more fascinating you are. Which, however, is not to imply that fascinating people blast through one conversational subject after another.

It merely means that the deeper down your knowledge goes, the greater your conversational *pow-uh.*

FASCINATING PEOPLE DON'T CONFORM

Independent thought is by definition nonconformity.

Conformity is about as boring and banal as it gets.

Fascinating people have the confidence to think for themselves.

Boring people do not.

Fascinating people like variety.

Boring people prefer the same old.

Conformity is the same old.

It is also the opposite of courageous. Because it takes courage to respond to conformity, as it takes courage to break away from the pack.

It takes courage to think for oneself.

If you're one of these rare courageous people, the world will certainly be held by you.

· · ·

FASCINATING PEOPLE ARE ESSENTIALLY **active and driven and disciplined**

Boring people are passive.

Discipline is a habit, and habit is a choice.

This is precisely why no one is fated to be boring — not even close.

How, then, does one go about expunging inveterate vapidity?

Certain studies I've seen show that you can bore people in two fundamental ways: both in *what* you say and in *how* you say it.

Being boring, in other words, can be an issue of subject-matter and style. Combine those two things into one and it's downright soporific.

The qualities that make a human fascinating, understand, or beguiling, or hypnotizing, or mesmerizing are — and this is important — a side-effect. They are a by-product: a by-product of a life lived well, a life lived *interestingly*. Thus the real insight into the power of fascination is this:

To be interesting is to be interested.

The fascinating person is not living her life to *be* fascinating: she's living her life, rather, in a way that cultivates her living potential, and this is why age cannot wither her, nor custom stale her infinite variety.

Because make no mistake: there are in the universe an infinite variety of fascinating things upon which you may fix your attention.

To be fascinating, therefore, you must come to recognize life as the adventure it is, and then proceed accordingly: live the adventure.

To be interesting is, I repeat, to be interested.

You must crave new experiences and desire a deeper understanding of the world.

Decide what you want and figure out how to get it.

Boring people don't have big dreams. They actually believe it when they're told, as we all are at one time or another, that they probably can't achieve their dreams.

Fascinating people, upon the other hand, believe no such thing.

Fascinating people shoot for the stars — and often reach them. And if they don't reach them, they become incontrovertibly more fascinating just in their singleminded striving.

Fascinating people picture their lives as they want their lives to be, and then they focus their energy on shaping their lives in that way.

Don't let others decide your future for you. Don't give people that kind of control over you. This is not only *not* fascinating: it's fatal.

Be the master of your own fate. Be the captain of your own soul — because, in the final analysis, fascinating people are the shapers of their own soul.

And that is why they seem to others not fractured but whole.

HOW TO BE UNFORGETTABLE

MOST PEOPLE ARE RELATIVELY FORGETTABLE. Not you.

Why?

Because you broke away from the pack a long time ago. You're a different breed — a dog of a different color.

You cultivated the black art of individuality, learned the art of personality. You became brilliant. People argue about your modesty.

She does things differently, they say, she's hetero-dox, self-contained, haunting the higher eminences of thought, hard-worker, school-leaver, reposed, self-taught.

Like all of us, she's a tightly packed pod of living potential, but she's EXPLODING: a life-giving force, a mustard seed.

She's never in need.

She has the common touch. Yet, som
remains pure and remote and above the fray.

She has a certain way.

She's silent. She's sensible.

She's sane.

She's generous.

She's still.

She's esoteric.

She's inquisitive.

She's independent.

She knows that self-development is the aim of life and that self-control is the basis of character.

She's happy.

She's not sloppy.

It takes a certain kind of work to be boring, whereas in order to be interesting it's ... what?

It's mostly a question of habit — and the true secret of habit, as everyone knows, is the insight that habit is discipline and that your habits are what you choose them to be: because your life is your values, and your values are what you most love and enjoy doing.

In this sense, your values become your habits.

***

UNFORGETTABLE PEOPLE CULTIVATE **their desire for knowledge**

t home in any public house,
oon, salon, or bar.

he unstoppable learning beast
t you know you are.

...ralizing. Specialize, yes, absolutely that too, but read a little about a lot — or, if you don't like to read, listen:

Enroll in a course. Attend a lecture. Plug into a podcast. Take in a play.

Most importantly: seek to integrate the new things you learn into the full body of your existing knowledge. In this way, your web of learning becomes interconnected, contextual, hierarchical, sweeping.

UNFORGETTABLE PEOPLE HAVE LEARNED **the lost art of listening**

You heard me right. (Or did you?)

People love to hear themselves talk, don't they? Not you. You're far too interesting for that. You're far too self-contained.

Attentive listening is an infallible hallmark of magnetism and good manners — which two things go together like whiskey and wieners.

By being an excellent listener, slow to speak and swift to hear, you'll go far in developing a kind of terrible fascination.

Brilliant listeners focus sincerely on what the other person is saying. They're curious.

They never participate in a conversation with the mindset that they'll listen only until it's their turn to talk.

If the whole time you're listening, you're thinking about what you're going to say next, it will show.

If you're fidgety, it will show.

In your patience possess ye your souls.

Patience and presence — being attentive — these are signals of strong listeners.

Strong listeners do this:

Pause before they respond.

Never interrupt.

Allow in total silence people to interrupt them.

UNFORGETTABLE PEOPLE ARE OFTEN **passionate storytellers**

There's a fairly simple way to become a passionate storyteller, and that's to create stories around subjects about which you're truly passionate.

If the subject-matter of your story is something you're genuinely interested in, your personality will irrepressibly shine through.

"As all art springs from personality, so it is only *to* personality that it can be revealed," wrote Oscar Wilde — and continued:

"There is no mood or passion that [the storyteller] cannot give us, and those who have discovered her secrets can settle beforehand what our experiences are going to be."

CHAPTER TITLE:

HOW TO BE UNFORGETTABLE

MOST PEOPLE ARE BORING.
NOT YOU.
WHY?
BECAUSE YOU BROKE AWAY FROM
THE PACK A LONG TIME AGO.
YOU'RE A DIFFERENT BREED - A
DOG OF A DIFFERENT COLOR...

YOU CULTIVATED THE BLACK ART
OF INDIVIDUALITY, LEARNED
THE ART OF PERSONALITY. YOU
BECAME BRILLIANT. PEOPLE
ARGUE ABOUT YOUR MODESTY.

SHE DOES THINGS DIFFERENTLY,
THEY SAY, SHE'S HETERODOX,
SELF-CONTAINED, HAUNTING THE
HIGHER EMINENCES OF THOUGHT,
HARD-WORKER, SCHOOL-LEAVER,
REPOSED, SELF-TAUGHT.

HOW TO BE THE SMARTEST PERSON
IN THE BAR

You can spot her from a mile away, the smartest person in the bar — or, if not quite from a mile, nonetheless from very far.

She doesn't necessarily think of herself as smart.

Still, her brain is carefully crafted — self-crafted and stylized — like a work of art.

Her eyes are alert and bright and lively. They twinkle.

She's relaxed and polite, with a well-modulated voice that speaks to you in the appropriate tone.

Her smile glows like expensive stone.

You do not quickly forget that smile.

She walks purposefully, and yet not aggressively, or with an overbearing style.

She has a sense of humor.

You can see that she knows there's a kind of

dignity in loneliness. She doesn't go out of the way to seek friends or groups or any kind of crowd.

In general she prefers quiet to loud.

She gives and receives compliments gracefully, can be strong and assertive, quick to stick up for herself, yet she can also speak of her shortcomings and accomplishments with an equal ease which you envy.

When communication or clarification is called for, she's never dismissive or inexplicably silent — never, of course, in any way aggressive or violent.

What's her trick?

What's her secret?

Her secret is this:

Develop a total disregard for where you think your abilities end.

Aim beyond what you believe you're capable of.

Do things you think you're not able to do.

Nothing is impossible, in this regard. The will to actually do it is the most important factor in becoming what you want.

The discipline to follow through is next. It is also the most difficult.

Why?

Why most difficult?

Because it requires relentless effort. It requires hour-after-hour, day-after-day practice.

It requires diligence.

Unless you're in a technical discipline like law or

medicine or mechanical engineering, drop out of college.

College stifles creativity.

It stunts the mind.

College is conformity — and the cost of conformity is colossal.

Individuality, on the other hand, is a prerequisite of genius, which, in turn, is the cultivation of your living potential.

The deeper your cultivation, the deeper your genius.

Cultivate, therefore, a durable purpose around which you can construct your life.

Purpose is largely willed: the more you do something, the deeper your understanding of it grows, so that after time your passion for that thing becomes hotter and then develops momentum and force, like a growing wave of water.

Whatsoever thy hand findest to do, do it with all thy might.

Seek to pay attention — seek it as a way of life. Attention is observation. It is light. Attention is the very seat of human will: the fundamental choice we face, all day, everyday, is the choice to pay attention or not. To be attentive is to be alert.

What, after all, does it mean to be smart?

It means, I repeat, to self-stylize your brain, like a work of art.

It means to observe the universe around you, as

well as the one within: to introspect, as thoughtful people do.

It means to be intelligent, like you.

Intelligence is your capacity to process a wide range of thoughts and ideas.

Which is perhaps why it never mattered to you when you were voted least likely to succeed — why it never fazed you when they called you a misfit, a malcontent, alienate, disaffiliate, deviant, recalcitrant — perhaps also why your natural-born predilections and proclivities and predispositions are and always have been to you essentially irrelevant: because intelligence is an *acquired* skill.

It must be developed by each person's own desire and activated by each person's will.

It must be habituated and automated by each person's own mind.

Which is why it's timeless and beautiful, and rather difficult to find.

This, incidentally, is true for both children and adults: the cultivation of intelligence requires effort — or, to put the same point in a slightly different way: thinking is an act of choice.

Thought requires work.

Whereas to be stoopid is relatively simple: all you have to do, in essence, is do nothing. If you do nothing, stoopid will naturally occur.

Being smart, however, requires a different sort of action.

It is not passive.

On the contrary, thinking is an entirely active process the undertaking of which is, when you consider it at all, massive.

She is intelligent, yes, but in a highly unorthodox way (they say) hard to pinpoint why: bookish but not book-smart, introspective, certainly, and everything she does — yes, everything — she does with all her heart.

One of my all-time favorite pieces of napkin-art. It was done for me by an artist named Mike, who knows well my love of books and literature.

THE TRUCKDRIVER

THE TRUCKDRIVER who lives next door is seldom home.

He's a long-haul trucker, he's over-the-road. He earns good money and does not spend. There's something ascetical about him, something wise. He's forty-nine. His hair is long. He wears jeans and combat boots. Sallow and haggard, his face is handsome nevertheless. His willowy wife does not ride with him but stays at home. They have no children. The wife is solitary, long-legged and tan. She has a pretty ponytail of sandy-brown. She smokes Marlboros. They do not rent but own. The wife spends hours in her garden, or she reads in her backyard. Her eyes are pensive. She waves to me but rarely speaks.

The trucker who lives next door arrives at unexpected hours, on unexpected days. Emerging from his rig, he has the leanness of a desert prophet about him. I imagine him eating very little while he's out on the road. He transports the goods from north-to-south. He hauls the freight from coast-to-coast. He kisses his wife of willow in the driveway. They hold hands and enter their tidy cottage together. They shut the door behind.

Sometimes, on holidays, his rig will sit for three or four consecutive nights along the residential side street where we live. It sits huge and gleaming in the dark. The trucker loves his rig: it is his home away from home. Once, well past two in the morning, coming in after a long bartending shift, I heard a gentle noise on my left and turned to look. The trucker who lives next door was polishing his semi in the moonlight. His semi is midnight-blue and chrome.

Here on the ragged edge of this desert town where the ancient railroad tracks lie rusting in the grass, the frontiers begin. These are the frontiers the trucker crosses and re-crosses year round. This town is like many western towns, with its looping river and cauliflower clouds, its one Masonic lodge and the hard clean skies above, and in the distance, fields of clay where woolly mammoth and dinosaur once knelt down in the soft earth to die, and a billion bison bones fossilize in the ground.

Beyond the backyards, the interstate curves off into the intricate horizon, and the distant cars make very little sound.

THE ART OF INDEPENDENT
THINKING

INDIVIDUALISM IS the act of thinking for yourself. It's rooted in the most fundamental choice you've got: the choice to pay attention or not.

There are approximately one thousand arguments against individualism — and every single one of them, without exception, is predicated upon a faulty premise.

That human beings are, for instance, essentially social doesn't negate or contradict our individualistic nature.

True individualism is not "rugged" — and the next time you hear that, dismiss it immediately for exactly what it is: a canard, if ever there was one.

Karl Marx saw humanity as an "organic whole," and people still like to use that stale phrase, pointing out simultaneously the obvious fact that "most humans grow up in families and live in societies." All of which misses the point entirely and does not render individualism void:

Individualism does not mean atomism.

Neither does it mean that humans are anti-social by nature.

Individualism doesn't necessarily embrace self-destructive hedonism, or moral subjectivism, or moral relativism, or fleeting pleasures that are too short-sighted to consider long-term consequences — or any of the other many adversary ethics that nullify human happiness over an entire lifespan.

Ultimately, the thing which grounds individualism in fact is that no one person can think for another — certainly not for a lifetime:

Only the individual reasons.

Only the individual thinks.

Thought is the fundamental act of human will.

When you distill it down to its essence, the decision to pay attention or not is the choice that determines all your other choices because it's what determines your thoughts.

For this reason it's not an exaggeration to say that the locus of free will is in the choice to pay attention or not.

We are each defined by our actions, and our actions are shaped by our thoughts.

The choice to focus your attention is the spark that ignites everything else because that initial choice is what shapes our thinking patterns.

Thinking is the uniquely human method of survival.

Thinking is reasoning.

Reason is the power of the human brain to form connections and make distinctions — which is to say: reason is the human capacity to discover the *identity* of things. Reasoning is the process of learning the nature of reality. It is the power to conceptualize. It is the process of learning what things are.

Recognizing this will take you far.

"Reason is also choice," said John Milton.

This insight — and what it implies — is the fundamental thing that makes individualism true.

Societies, communities, tribes, bands, and so forth — they are all and only composed of individuals, each one of whom must perform alone, in the privacy of her or his own mind, the fundamental thing that shapes every subsequent thing:

Each individual must choose to focus the brain and pay attention, or not. It is a choice we each face every waking hour of every day, like a continual and yet not unpleasant kind of quiz.

That is where the art of individuality begins, and ends: in the most essential choice there is.

HIGH-SCHOOL BASKETBALL STAR

You were a pure shooter, a long shot. You were a star.

Just another nobody boy, half-black, half-white, raised in a fractured home in middle America: a drunk father who worked twenty-five years for Clayton County, and a mother who loved you but was always too passive, it seemed, to truly care.

Yet you were inherently happy. Your smile exploded across your face like a star-shell. Happiness was in your bones, your blood, your ectomorphic body, not tall, but an arrant athlete from head to toe.

The college coaches all went crazy for you, but your test scores were poor. You never quite made the grade. You served instead as an infantry solider in the first desert war: a gunner, a dead-eye.

When you shook the high-school rafters that

late-autumn night, scoring seventy-eight points, shooting twenty-for-twenty in the second half, both sides of the bleachers erupting for your grace, the purity of your touch, your form and joy, the achievement of — the mastery of the thing — oh, you were beautiful.

When you won the 100 meters and then the 200 against all the big-city boys, edging out by fractions, in both races, two future Olympians, your heart as big as the ocean — you were beautiful.

When, at thirty-three, you lied about your age and landed a tryout with the Denver Nuggets and made it down to the final cut, still going strong, still a gunner, a dead-eye, with ice-water in the veins, your untouchable happiness like star-shine all around you, love of sport, love of body-in-motion, and still a sniper from the three-point line, but then busted your ankle in a fall — even then you were beautiful too.

And are you beautiful still in your oil-stained clothes, turning wrenches at the garage, your thin black fingers spiderlike among the parts? Do you still have that delicate touch?

Are you beautiful with your scuffed-up knuckles and your immutable smile, your snaggly teeth and skeletal face, your elegant hands that lift the tumbler of whiskey at my Sunday night bar, a calm and generous guest, unfailingly polite to me and to everyone, eyes closed in concentration while you listen to the jazz piano — studying those notes with pure precision played, the virtuosity you fully recognize, and fully admire?

Are you beautiful in your worn-out hightop sneakers and that jumpsuit mechanic uniform, your chocolate slab of forelock hanging lank across your cheek?

Are you beautiful in your small hometown, moving into middle-age, still so thin, so graceful-looking, filling in part-time at the cowboy hat store? Is your uncanny coordination fading with disuse? Your unbelievable speed and balance, your infallible sense of direction and time?

I saw you once, not long ago, drinking coffee from a styrofoam cup on the fire escape of your apartment building. It was mid August, peak of the Perseids. You stood at the rail in a white tanktop and pleated gray slacks. You looked aristocratic — flat-stomached and lean, handsome. The day was dying. The trees beyond stood iron-black against the sky. The staircases along the outer buildings were duplicated in isometric shadows across the orange brick walls. I was visiting a woman who lived across the street, and I watched you from her kitchen window. Soon you sat down and looked at the sky. You sipped your coffee and sat there for a long time upon the metal steps. The sky flared burgundy, blood-red. Then it drained away into a reef of green. You watched. Darkness came. The first stars appeared.

Still you sat. You sat and sat, and after a while, the stars began streaming across the sky: stars everywhere and more stars, stars rocketing down the arc of the firmament, corridors of molten matter now come alive in a physical radiance so pure and energetic that it seemed to contain the essence of brightness itself — brightness and beauty, wild cosmic beauty illuminating the heavens and earth below with its rare and shooting light.

BEWARE OF DOGMA

THE DIFFERENCE between dogma and doctrine is the difference between faith and thought. The extent to which an ideological system is taken on faith is the extent to which it is dogmatic. The extent to which an ideological system is by its spokespeople *expected* to be taken on faith is the extent to which it is dogma proper.

Accepting an ideological system without actually grasping or understanding the system's ideological roots and elaborations — its claims, tenets, and principles — is ultimately the thing that distinguishes the dogmatic from the non-dogmatic.

Ideas and claims and principles accepted upon faith, even if they're accurate, though without one's having independently thought about and considered the principles *in toto* (and thus not having fully grasped them), are dogmatically held principles.

Cults are among the most obvious examples of dogma-in-action, but it is important to note that neither religion nor God nor supernaturalism are the distinguishing characteristics of dogma. Any ideology, religious or non-religious, can become dogmatic, and some of the most notorious dogmas in history have been secular — Marxism perhaps foremost among them all, certainly in terms of the sheer numbers of people killed and imprisoned in the name of it.

What delineates and separates the dogmatic from the non isn't primarily falsehood versus truthhood, but rather the level of independent examination which any one individual adherent gives to the ideological system, and the individual's subsequent grasp, or lack.

A system of beliefs, whether true or false, becomes dogma when the preponderance of adherents accept it upon faith and when such is expected of them by those in positions of leadership or authority.

Dogma exists along a spectrum. It is for this reason possible to be "somewhat dogmatic," as it is also possible to be "extremely dogmatic," as it is also possible to be at points in between.

"When we blindly adopt a religion, a political system, a literary dogma, we become automatons," wrote Anaïs Nin, sagely, and her words, in my opinion, capture the essence of dogma.

"You are rather dogmatic in your espousal of atheism, Mr. Shermer," said a caller on the radio to Michael Shermer, publisher of *Skeptic Magazine.*

I agree with this caller as well: atheism has undoubtedly, within many circles, become a dogma, fully fledged, and under the label of "new atheism," the atheist dogma (i.e. the "new-atheist movement") went to a whole new level of atheistic dogmatism – that is, before losing most of its momentum, in no small measure because of the dogmatic political-economic views which new atheism came to adopt as part of their package, and which political-economic views consist largely of the standard progressive-liberal ideology of today: instant dismissal and hatred of anyone on "the right," for instance, as well as a deep advocacy of state-forced altruism and compulsory egalitarianism. This became new-atheism's politico-ethical code, and it is a significant part of the platform now, a la Richard Dawkins and Sam Harris, two of its biggest spokesmen.

Many atheists argue that atheism provides its own protection against dogma. Atheism is on principle opposed to faith, they say, and therefore any attempt to take atheistic principles on faith cannot be done. I agree that atheism doesn't require faith — and I often hear believers incorrectly charge that atheism is just another sort of faith (it is not) — yet I still think the atheist argument isn't accurate:

atheism does not, in my opinion, provide its own protection against dogma, inasmuch as any system of beliefs, even scientific, must undergo deep scrutiny, which means that proponents must individually put forth the effort required in order to critically examine and understand the system. If and as far as this isn't done while yet proclaiming the truth of the doctrine, it is dogmatic.

A system of beliefs, whether accurate or inaccurate, becomes a dogma when the preponderance of proponents do what I've just described — and, even more, when the official spokespeople for it replace reasoning with militancy and any kind of decrees from or of authority: things expected a person either accept or obey — or the person is a heretic.

I regard this subject as complex. The determining factor, I'll reiterate, is the extent to which the belief-system is blindly propounded, and blindly accepted.

It almost goes without saying here that not all atheists are dogmatists – just as not all Marxists are dogmatists, just as not all religious people are dogmatists.

Some of the most learned and genuinely intelligent and well-educated people to whom I've ever had the pleasure of speaking are religious — one, a Catholic priest named Father Schmidt, was a doctor of philosophy, theology, and psychology. He was also a calm and exceptionally erudite man, with a scintillating sense of humor, witty, laid-back, an occasional drinker at a bar I once tended, and I learned a lot from him, and *definitely* no dogmatist was he. He was the opposite, in fact, and he and our conversations meant a great deal to me.

This issue can be no better illustrated than in the fact that if any self-described liberal-democrat (among the most dogmatic of people with whom I regularly come in contact now, which is why I single them out here for illustrative purposes) were to entirely divest himself or herself of partisan political dogma, even for a short time, and replace it with a sincere and deep examination of any number of economic claims made by garden-variety conserva- tives — how price controls create shortages, for instance, or how minimum wage laws create greater unemployment — this same self-described liberal- democrat, if sincere in his or her critical examina- tion, *would* indeed see that many of these main- stream conservative economic claims are accurate, the progressive-democrats inaccurate.

Militant atheists *aussi:* they are invariably among the most intolerant of all dogmatists I routinely come across – two I know personally going so far as to say that Issac Newton and Galile Galileo, both of whom believed in God, were necessarily "lesser" than, for instance, Brad Pitt, who is atheist! (My incredulity, I assure you, is nothing against Brad Pitt.)

The error here — an obvious error, to be sure —

is in placing all or even most moral merit upon the notion that belief in God is a fundamental virtue. It is not.

There's much more to human virtue and human life, and billions of excellent people believe in God, and, let us also never forget: *caritas* maketh up for the multitude of wrongs, because *caritas,* like benevolence, kindness, *agape,* is a fundamental virtue, gentle, patient, compassionate, timeless.

Think of dogma this way:

It is a system of beliefs arranged and organized and placed into a tidy-looking bundle, which is made of wet clay. In accepting the bundle, one accepts as well, by necessity — by virtue of what dogma is — all the items packaged inside, and those items, too, are each made of wet clay. Often it happens that in the course of unpackaging the bundle, one finds a number of things unexpected inside – items not necessarily loved or even liked. And yet these items *are* a part of the totality. The longer you keep the bundle as your own, the more the wet clay hardens — until, eventually, this clay is no longer wet or damp but completely solidified.

It is, to further firm-up the point, simple for one to refer to oneself as an "environmentalist" — yet how many notions and ideas and assumptions are subsumed under and bundled within that simple-to-say ideological title: vast sequence-chains and theories, complicated interpretations of data, much of which data is incomplete and incompletely gathered — so much, in fact, that one is very hard-pressed indeed to meet any self-described environmentalist who has gone to the trouble and effort of closely investigating the innumerable theories that undergird the environmental ideology. Yet who would want to come out as explicitly anti-environmentalism?

The same could be said about any number of other isms — and this doesn't even touch upon the subject of all the divisions and disagreements and subdivisions *within* any of these isms; nor the sects and sub-sects and interminable schisms, which in turn spawn more dogmas, which in turn spawn more isms.

Nor does it touch upon the *deliberate* prevarications and misrepresentations — the propagandistic "over-representation of factual presentations on how dangerous it is," as Albert Gore so famously expressed it, "as a predicate for opening up the audience to listen to what the solutions are." (Unquote.) He and all the others know full well that the *overwhelming* majority of people who hear these "over-representations" are going to believe these dogmas entirely, with no qualms or questions asked, no scruples, no independent thought given, without so much as a glance into actual data which would shed light onto these tenets of pure dogmatism. He knows also that these same people will then make it their life mission to convert the rest of the world to their apocalyptic platform and vision.

A person can spend his or her life combatting such things.

I write about dogma at length here because it's a subject I've thought and thought about, beginning as early as my early teenage years, and I still think a great deal about it — even more now, for this chapter and book. The subject is intricate, labyrinthian.

"Rejoice in the truth, and let all your things be done with *caritas*," I believe it says somewhere in the first Corinthian.

It also, in a very significant way, strikes at the heart of the subject-matter of independent thinking as an art.

It strikes at the heart of the subject-matter because dogma as I've come to understand it and define it here is the very antithesis of independent thought, which is also critical thought: a critical examination of ideas and ideologies, almost as a way of life.

Dogma is dangerous. It is an attempt to circumvent the process of thought — to short-cut the effort that thinking requires. It erects barriers to independent thought, puts stumbling-blocks in the way of individual inquiry. It creates division and strife.

Critical Race Theory (CRT) is a current case in point. I say that because it's most definitely dogma, and, if nothing else, the CRT acronym instantly gives it away. (Jargon and dogma go together like white wine and fish.)

#BlackLivesMatter is dogma. You may have my blood in a dish.

Environmentalism, I repeat, is pure dogma — pure and unadulterated: it is dogma piled on top of dogmatism. That is environmentalism.

Climate change, an environmental offshoot and schism, is also dogma, insofar as the term "climate change" is so imprecise as to be virtually meaningless since climate is non-static by definition (sloppy terminology is a dead giveaway, by the way — always and unfailingly a foolproof sign of dogmatic supposition and presupposition). I know of no serious scientist or human being who doesn't understand that climate changes by definition — that the 1980's were not earth's optimum temperature — and yet how many from all walks of life use the term, clinging to it with blind passion and so much sanctimony and zeal, totally moved, wielding the term with dogmatic fervor and force. Meanwhile, there have never, in recorded history, been fewer climate-related deaths than in the last decade, of course. This can be proved.

And no discussion of dogma would be complete right now if I were to neglect mentioning the thing which in many ways was the hook that yanked my brain painfully enough to provoke this book. I'm referring, as you would suspect, to the ideology that's sprung up around SARS-CoV2 — complete with its own lingo as well, its own acronym-set, its own jargon and nomenclature, all of which became dogmatic in a shorter span of time than anything we've ever seen, I'll bet.

Thought — true thought, and not a bundle of hardening clay beliefs — is the only real antidote to dogma, because true thought is investigative by definition, as it is also inquisitive by its very nature.

WHAT IS FRIENDSHIP?

THE BEAUTIFUL JAPANESE word *kenzoku* connotes a chemistry or a bond sourced in similarity of spirit. It suggests the sharing of certain core values.

It is in this sense that our most profound connections come from our power of choice — not birth or blood — because our values are chosen and developed by each one of us individually.

In a fundamental sense, friendship comes from our capacity to value.

Valuing is an individual choice. It stems from our thoughts.

Our values are our desires and passions.

Our desires and passions are willed.

Those who value things most deeply, feel love most deeply.

Friendship exists along a spectrum: there are

different degrees, types, and depths. And yet they all have one thing in common:

They're all founded upon esteem and affection for another person.

Friendship is reciprocal.

The friends whom you feel the most affection for are the friends who reflect your deepest values.

You needn't even have very much in common with your closest friends: provided you're like-minded in certain *fundamental* things — this, more than any other thing, will bond you at the most fundamental level.

Love is in this way mirror-like: it reflects those values you yourself hold most dear.

"Natural love is nothing more than the fundamental inclination which is stamped upon every being by the Author of nature," wrote Thomas Aquinas.

Like his teacher Aristotle, Aquinas believed that the highest love was friendship.

Both, however, believed that friendship was just a precursor to understanding the love that is, in Aquinas's words, *caritas*.

One of the first questions Aquinas poses in his tract on caritas is whether it equals friendship. He answers this way:

*According to Aristotle (**Ethics VIII, 4**) not all love has the character of friendship, but only that love which goes with wishing well, namely when we so love another as to* *will what is good for him. For if we do not will what is good to the things we love but rather, we will their good for ourselves, as we are said to love wine, a horse or the like, then that is not love of friendship but a love of desire. For it would be foolish to say that someone has friendship with wine or a horse.*

But benevolence alone does not suffice to constitute friendship; it also requires a certain mutual loving, because a friend is friendly to his friend. But such mutual benevolence is based on something shared in common.

Both Aquinas and Aristotle believed that love is *active*.

When there ceases to be an active and passionate mind, there ceases to be values.

When there ceases to be values, the capacity for friendship is proportionately diminished.

Love and friendship are both life-affirming and also life-giving: they are an interplay of mirror-like reflection and exchange. And they both begin with the individual's capacity to value.

Life is largely a process of valuing.

And valuing begins — and ends — in the individual mind.

"WHISKEY IS MERELY SUNSHINE HELD TOGETHER BY WATER"

IT WAS a mistaken message that started it all: a mysterious text sent to her number in the deepest part of the lonely night — her phone, face-up across her lap, all at once coming to life with a soundless throb of silvery light.

Later, when she shuffled back through the slender deck of cards which were the events of this night, she wasn't surprised to discover that she remembered everything with an almost dreamlike clarity: alone in her flat, laying low on a Friday night, not sleeping but seated upon her bedroom floor and listening to piano chords seep through the speakers of her stereo, a gentle click of rain just beginning — and then that first cryptic message in a bloom of electronic light.

She happened to just then be looking in the direction of her phone, almost as though she'd been waiting after all — almost, indeed, as though in her music-addled melancholy fog she'd wanted it to come — and, tilting her head like a dog (her phone still face-up across her lap) but otherwise unmoving, she read:

"Some say whiskey is merely sunshine held together by water."

This is what the message said.

Through her rain-stippled windowpane and across the alleyway, not far below her second-story flat, she saw the only other light around her now wink out (her neighbor, the late-night barman whom she barely knew, though liked). Watery darkness descended all about her like a shout.

She knitted her brows and, baffled but also intrigued, she read the message again. And then again. It was clearly a mistake, yet she felt herself pulled in and almost instantly immersed. A second message, then — coming from the same mysterious source — appeared below the first:

"Some of us are followers. Some of us are leaders. These are just the facts. This book is for leaders, of course."

She wasn't quite finished reading this missive when a third one unexpectedly bloomed:

"Yet none in life are fated, are they?"

There was a longer pause while she read and read again. Then a longer one came in:

"No human is truly slotted into some unalterable

place or role, some fixed unchosen path. Excellence is not a rarified DNA strand reserved only for a selected few. Me. You. Our lives are all cultivated, yes. Yes. All. I believe that this is true. Conformists can unconform. Followers, if they want, can learn to lead — lead by example, best of all: leaders, learners, free-thinkers, nonconformists, anything we want with enough passion and zeal. Do you think this is true? Of course no one need to if they don't want it, and there's nothing wrong in this. Still, I think followers who grasp the core of the book, its meaning and its theme, will do more than merely — you know — 'dare to dream.' Because there is no darkness but ignorance, and the price of wisdom is above rubies."

Then the messages ceased.

She felt perhaps the neural itch of inkling now. Talking lit while getting lit. And now her hanging heart beat fast — hammering inexplicably against the cherry-walls of her cavernous chest. The blood-gush through her veins increased. "May I know who this is?" she wrote at last, tapping deftly with her thumbs.

After sending which, though, there was only silence — silence and a sudden sense of stillness that she couldn't explicitly codify or name. It frightened her. Yet also a lingering tremor of intent still flickering from the words — their words — living words, the product of their thinking brains, the words they'd each already sent. Her face glowed greenly phosphorescent in the room. Outside the gentle rain decreased, died.

Thus she waited. Thus she stared. She eyed with lidless fixity her pulsing cell-phone screen. She watched with a gaze of liquid heat. Abruptly, then, and to her horror, her phone went black. Simultaneous to that, the piano music ceased. Silence was complete. Still she waited. Still she stared. She stared into the wild darkness of her screen as upon the darkness across the face of the deep where the spirit of primeval God did move and creep. She didn't shift — neither shift nor fidget nor twitch. The darkness around her grew velveteen fur, the silence evolving into a complex thing, imponderable, rich. The moment she felt herself about to burst, a mini miracle occurred: the electronic light bloomed back with life, keeping the darkness at bay — light and life in the written words of a sapient power-source. She nearly gasped.

"Sorry," the message said. She thought it carried a note of real regret. "I thought I knew who. Wrong person. Please forgive, forget."

Immediately she started typing a reply, but a second message interrupted this silent typing work, a message coming in through a narrow cleft or corridor of night:

"The word 'wisdom' is a derivative of the word 'wit,'" it said, "which I didn't know before I read this book. I, however, am nothing more than a half-witted tool."

Again she started to reply when yet a third message danced before her eyes — her eyes alight now and glowing like pools of greenish-red:

"Goodbye and goodnight," the dancing message said.

"Stranger ..." she swiftly wrote, and touched the upward arrow that signifies to send.

She at once typed another message, a sense of urgency mixed with something like longing — now awakened within her and now growing rapidly acute: "Fellow pilgrim of the night ..." She touched the send again.

There was no reply. Nothing at all. Nothing except stillness — stillness and a silence that reigned: cosmic, absolute, the foothold of the night regained.

"Pilgrim?" she wrote, yet with no real hope in what was now the slushy snowcone of her cherry-colored heart. Nor did she in that moment hear the silence softly break outside as the rain began anew, with a sound like the whisper of wind in the grass, and the front door across the way opened, with a gentle snick and rasp. She tapped the upward arrow once again.

And then something unexpected happened — something that struck her as an amazing, magical thing:

Almost instantly, as if poised there with equivalent longing in the darkness of the void, the following message came:

"Yes?" the stranger's message said.

Her scalp went numb, hot needles raining down upon her head. But then nothing more.

Until the gentle knock upon her door:

The one she secretly hoped would come.

WHAT IS INDEPENDENT THINKING?

INDEPENDENT THINKING IS YOU, your car, and an auto-mechanic you don't really know.

Independent thinking is you taking your car in for a biannual tune-up, strictly routine. After handing the auto-mechanic your car keys and then waiting in the lobby for approximately five minutes, this same mechanic comes into the lobby and says to you:

"Your oil is pretty dirty and it's also getting low. I recommend an oil-change, which I can and will do right now for $25.00. It will take me about ten minutes."

Observe yourself sincerely in this scenario.

Consider what you personally would be thinking in that situation.

Not everybody would process this information the same, and that's part of the point: because individual evaluation and the importance which each individual assigns to a given piece of information determines, more often than not, the degree of independent thought.

The primary factors are each individual context-of-knowledge and each value-structure contained within each individual person.

So: you may or may not check the dipstick yourself — to observe the oil-level firsthand and to see how dirty it looks to you, depending, perhaps, on how much you know about cars and dipsticks and oil-levels and the look of new oil versus old oil, and depending also on how much you care about your time and a "measly" — or precious — $25.00.

Or perhaps you've already deliberated over this particular thing, before you even got here, because you already assumed you needed an oil-change, based strictly upon the amount of time that's passed since your last oil change. Perhaps you even have a soft little sticker on the top-left inside of your windshield telling you when you need an oil change, and perhaps you've been paying close attention to that little sticker.

Or perhaps you've noticed that the exhaust coming out of your tailpipe is whiter in color than it used to be. Or perhaps you think of a specific thing that your mother or father (or your brother or sister or your roommate or your boyfriend or your girlfriend) said to you about your car and your oil.

Or perhaps you think of something else entirely that doesn't even occur to me here. This is only meant to analogize — to concretize the nature of independent thinking and how it operates for all individual human beings. I realize more than ever now, in writing this book and driving deeper into the subject than I've done to date, that the issues are, on one hand, more complex than some people would have it – yet, at the same time, they're also not as intractable as others make them out to be.

Independent thinking is *not* necessarily synonymous with original thinking, nor is it necessarily synonymous with contrary thinking, nor is it at all a question of brilliance or intelligence-quotient (so-called) or anything of that nature.

It is a fact, as well, that we all rely on people with specialized knowledge – everyday – and we all take plenty of people at their words, without questioning every single piece of every single bit of information that comes our way, moment-by-moment, hour-by-hour, day-by-day, year-in-year-out.

The primary principle is in individually *processing* or not processing information — depending largely upon one's context and one's value-hierarchy (i.e. what each individual person regards as important).

The independent thinker is nothing more or less than the person who assumes responsibility for the *ultimate* contents of her or his own mind. It is entirely possible for someone who is a genuinely thoughtful and independently thinking person to nonetheless take you at your word if you tell her some fact she's not particularly interested in: a new song by a musician she doesn't know or care about, for example.

After considering, then, how you'd process the information the auto-mechanic gives you about an oil-change, imagine that next, for whatever personal reasons, you tell the mechanic to proceed with the oil change.

"You need an air-filter change," the mechanic then says to you, halfway through the oil-change. "This will cost you another $25.00. But I have in the shop here the exact kind of air-filter your car requires, and it will only take me about sixty seconds to remove the old one and install the new one."

The mechanic then shows you your old air-filter, which perhaps you take a moment to look at and observe — or perhaps not.

You may or may not know how dirty the air-filter actually is, depending upon your past experiences and your context of knowledge concerning air-filters – specifically, I mean, in whether you have a gauge or standard of measurement by which to determine if an air-filter is very dirty, versus moderately dirty, versus barely dirty, versus clean. And so what do you do?

You may or may not call a friend or a family member, or you may or may not ask the mechanic questions, or you may or may not do a quick search on your phone – possibly watch a video about when to change your air-filter, or to pull up an image of what a dirty air-filter actually looks like.

Or perhaps you don't bother with any of that at all, and you just barely process what the mechanic said to you and you tell him to go ahead with the air-filter change as well — or perhaps you decided upon the very opposite of that: you barely think about what the mechanic said, barely paying attention to your air-filter when the mechanic shows it to you, and yet even so, you tell the mechanic *not* to change it, because no matter how dirty it may or may not actually be, you simply don't regard it as important.

If, however, you do nothing at all – not even glance at the air filter when the mechanic attempts to show it to you – but then nod in acquiescence and tell the mechanic to change it and charge you for it, observe what you're doing in that instance:

You're taking the auto-mechanic on faith.

Now imagine that many, many more things are presented to you by this mechanic: You might want to consider your transmission fluid, this mechanic says, and your power-steering fluid, brake fluid, anti-freeze.

Then imagine the mechanic bringing up other issues – things which are even more serious: Your muffler is about to fall off. Your battery is nearly dead. Your spark plugs are shot. Your fuel pump is going. Your transmission seems as though it might be about to die. Your electrical system is full of bad wiring. Your engine even sounds off and may need to be rebuilt. And so on.

Consider your personal reaction to all these hypothetical things — how you'd *think* about them, how you'd address them, one way or another — specifically, how much independent thought you'd put into each of them. Ask yourself: what determines how much thought and effort you're willing to put in? Is it your interest level?

And what, in turn, determines that?

Now use this same analogy but with your physical health: a doctor at your annual health check-up telling you several things which needs looking into. Consider how with your physical well-being you're almost certainly more motivated to deliberate in your own mind and then decide for yourself how much you'll investigate any, all, some, or none of the things you're being told. But once you've decided, how do you investigate and evaluate? How specifically do you check and re-check? What determines which issues you'll investigate more critically and with greater scrutiny?

If your condition is diagnosed as an urgent stage-three condition, which left untreated could kill you, would you go for a second or even third opinion? Would you research it to the utmost and learn as much as you possibly could? Would you choose a naturopathic practitioner for something like this, or would you choose, for instance, a world-class oncologist? Those questions are not put forth snidely but sincerely. Such a serious condition would almost surely, at the very least, by the majority of people, be investigated with greater depth and urgency than something diagnosed as "probably nothing."

Transfer this same basic process into the realm of politico-economic claims.

Transfer it into the realm of historic claims.

Transfer it into the realm of religious or philosophical claims.

What determines the degree of seriousness and importance?

Command and control?

The abrogation of politico-economic rights?

IN THE REALM of human cognition, all knowledge is shaped and conditioned by the structure of the human mind, which operates by means of reason, which, to quote Mr. Spinoza again, is "a faculty for the integration of knowledge, which human beings possess."

Different people care about different things, to be sure.

If, for example, a bartender says to you that the word "gin" is a shortened version of the word "genever" which comes from the Latin "juniperus" which refers to juniper, and this, the bartender says, goes far in explaining why the predominant flavor of gin is juniper berry – you may or may not take this bartender at her word, and you may or may not care, one way or the other. You may, on the one hand, be interested enough in this subject-matter to store that information in your mind (or perhaps even write it down), and then you may more thoroughly research it later. On the other hand, you may not.

Perhaps a professor tells you that the highest mountain in Mexico is a dormant volcano called Pico de Orizaba, and what do you personally do with that information? How much does it matter to you? Do you remember it? Do you integrate it with what you already know about any number of other things? Or does that particular piece of information go in one ear and out the — you know — other? What if this same professor then told you that under Mexico's highest mountain is one of the only remaining oil reserves left in North America, and that the entire planet's reserves of oil are barely enough to last five more years? Do you think about and remember what the professor said in this case? Or not? Do you merely take her at her word? Or do you begin investigating this issue for yourself?

Different people, I reiterate, respond differently to different things. There is no problem with this — that is, until it leads to decisions of serious politico-economic policies which violate individual sanctity.

. . .

THE BEAUTY of the transmission of knowledge, which is fostered by the division of labor, is that so many diverse ideas and facts from so many diverse people has created an exponential amplification of knowledge: different people interested in different facts and fields-of-study, any one of which when synthesized by the mind of another human being leads to a more profound understanding and depth of learning that surpasses what any of these different people possessed individually.

This is the essence of civilization and human progress.

Knowledge forms a unity. It is deeply interwoven and interconnected, as it is also hierarchical. As such, not all knowledge is equal in its hierarchical importance.

The main issue of present-day societal conflicts is not rightwing or leftwing, which in the scope of things is meaningless partisan quibbling. The main issue is whether humans should give away freedom, private initiative, and individual responsibility, and surrender it to the guardianship of a gigantic apparatus of compulsion.

There are two foolproof methods and measures by which to gauge the importance and necessity of independent thought:

First, matters of command-and-control over individual autonomy and the freedom to exchange.

Second, catastrophizing, which should always be looked upon suspiciously.

The art of independent thinking is the art of independently *processing* — processing, I emphasize, as distinguished from parroting without the mental effort and exertion of focus required to grasp and comprehend the meaning of the words one is using. *That* and that alone is the stuff of which independent thought consists.

Independent thinking is you, your car, and an auto-mechanic you don't really know, and it is what you then *choose* to do with the information presented to you.

THE WOMAN WITH THE
GRASSHOPPER MIND

"Every serious civilization, like every serious person, possesses an essence or a spirit," said the woman with the grasshopper mind. "A soul, if you like."

She was a political refugee standing – and not sitting – at my bar one quiet Tuesday evening. People called her the woman with the grasshopper mind, I wasn't entirely sure why, though I was shortly to find out. She was half Puerto Rican and half Cuban, born in Puerto Rico but raised in Cuba, her name Katya Reyes. Not tall, not particularly thin, no longer young, yet still strikingly attractive, she had the kind of beauty thrown into sharper relief by the sheer strength of her personality, her eloquence, the leaping nimbleness of her mind: a fierce and fearless brilliance that shone brightly in her liquid black eyes. She had a way, as well, of drawing people in – even those who disagreed with her – and this too was largely the result of her multilingual articulateness combined with an unapologetic independence of thought and heterodoxy of thinking.

She was not speaking to me but to a small group who had gathered near her – almost, it seemed, unconsciously so – one of whom, having attended a campus talk she'd given earlier that same day, had started her upon this conversation: by asking her in a friendly but provocative tone an unmistakably antagonistic question, the main thrust of which, after much divagation on this young questioner's part, was whether she supported the notion that slavery alone had built America. Katya Reyes continued in her reply:

"As the spirit of every individual human being is most authentically disclosed in the unconscious postures and gestures and expressions of each individual, so, too, is the spirit of every civilization most authentically expressed in the unconscious attitudes and actions" — she interrupted herself — "the mores and mannerisms," she said, "the *modus-vivendi* of its citizenry."

She paused long enough to sip honey-colored rum from the snifter in which I'd served it – a snifter nearly as large as her face, and the sheer size of which snifter made it particularly easy for an amateur like me to over-pour.

"This fundamental spirit," she said, swallowing

her mouthful of honeyed rum, "may be described as the essence of a culture, or … what did you call it in your book about the young Navajo runner, Mr. Bartender? That other word for essence? Quiddity, yes, that's right. A culture's quiddity may be defined as the composite of characteristics which form that culture's core – and by this I mean: the unconscious style and lifestyle of the people. This style is the outward expression of ideas that have been fully absorbed and yet tacitly so – tacitly and even unconsciously absorbed, I should say – ideas which may seem self-evident but which, in actuality, are the end result and *consequence* of a complicated synthesis of that society's dominant ideas: ideas about human existence and the individual's place in society. The sympatico Italians are an example of what I mean, or the proper English with their dry humors."

She paused again and sipped from her big bulbous snifter, which glowed so softly under the creamy bar lights.

"A country's politico-economic trends are the result of a long and chain-like sequence of ideas," Katya Reyes said. "They are also the equivalent of an individual's actions in practical reality. And just as an individual's stated beliefs can contradict the values she or he has subconsciously adopted, so, too, a country's quiddity can contradict its explicit policies."

She paused and took another sip of rum.

"Also," she continued, "just as it is psychologically dicey for any individual human being to neglect the task of consciously identifying the values she or he has come to subconsciously absorb, so for the same reason is it dicey for any country to ignore the ramifications of the policies the country has come to implicitly absorb. One thing is certain: the more insular a given society, the less context the youth have for evaluation and appraisal. Because, by virtue of living in that place and growing up among it all, the majority of young people do, in general, absorb the dominant ideas which ultimately go into shaping a given country or culture's quiddity."

She took a drink of water now and then chased it with another swallow of rum. She signaled me silently for a straw. Oh, she was doing quite well, I thought, her over-pour of rum, which I assessed while getting her straw, holding up nicely.

"America's quiddity," she said, and then paused, ostensibly to clear her throat of rum — and yet now I wonder a little if maybe she hadn't started to choke-up with some emotion, for she was as passionate a person as I'd ever come across, who grasped and therefore felt things deeply, authentically. "America's quiddity," she rebegan, "is independence."

This was in direct response to the original question — immediately upon saying which, however, many among this small gathering of people began to object and protest, in a rising crescendo of murmurs. But Katya Reyes, the refugee and woman with a grasshopper mind, her articulate speech laced so strongly still with her lilting Cubano and Puerto Rican, would not be gainsaid. She held up her hand in an authoritative gesture, and she spoke over the rising crescendo of murmurs:

"A moment, please," she said, not loudly and yet with great conviction. "I am well aware, my good people, of the faults and contradictions held by many of America's primary theoreticians and philosophical architects. My statement stands, and I am fully prepared to back it up. I was asked a question, and I request that you now please pay me the respect of listening to my full answer, and I ask also that you seek to understand the nature of historical context and its intricacies and nuances and the complexity of trying to capture this in a reasonably brief way while standing outnumbered at a bar. I repeat: America's quiddity is her spirit of independence – specifically, I mean the foundational idea that humans are self-sufficient and *more* efficacious without government intrusion. And no matter how egregiously this spirit of independence has been throttled or breeched and no matter how many contradictory views were held by the people who founded America, it is *still*, I say to you now, the essence of America, the soul of America, and it is precisely this essence and soul that must be fought for without rest, respite, surcease. America, unique among all civilizations across all human history, is the only civilization in human history that explicitly named, specified, and legally recognized the rights of each individual, which resulted in individual freedom from government authority at last: saying, in essence, humans do not exist and flourish merely by government permission but by natural-born right. This idea was implemented neither fully nor thoroughly nor perfectly, but the error — an abominable error, to be sure, which, I agree, should never be forgotten — was entirely in the *implementation* and not the principle itself. The principle remains immutable and true, and it is a prodigious accomplishment which should not be cheapened or taken lightly ... or forgotten. It should be remembered and respected over and above everything, in fact. Wait, please. I let you talk, young man, for quite some time, even while your question was a backhanded attack upon me — yes, I recognized it — and now it is my turn."

She paused and looked over the crystal rim of her snifter, and then she took another sip of rum, her wet black eyes bright and gleaming. She resumed:

"The spirit I speak of," she said, "is the *sole* reason that, even for all the contradictions and horrific breaches in America's history – slavery, the treatment of American aboriginals, the treatment of women, and everything else – America became, in the shortest span of time *by far,* the wealthiest and in many ways the greatest civilization in human history. This spirit alone is what made America, and it is also what saved America, because the ideas behind America's foundation won-out in a horrid and bloody civil war which killed approximately one million Americans, if you count civilians, all colors, all races, all sexes. They are the *only* ideas anywhere, ever, that can preserve human freedom. That is what I mean by 'immutable.'"

She looked across the room.

No one spoke.

"Americans were the first and only to break from the abhorrent ideology that had dominated human history since the dawn of humankind – an ideology which made slavery continuous and even common-place across all cultures, on every inhabited continent on the planet: the ideology that individuals *must* depend not on themselves but on an overarching authority in order to live, to prosper, to thrive, an authority which alone, it was believed and is still believed across most of the world, can grant us our well-being, so that when good happens, we owe it not to our own individual resourcefulness or personal initiative or self-motivated and self-sustaining drive and desire but solely to the bureaucratic powers that be, who grant us, God-like, permission to live, since our lives are not ours by right but only by permission. It is in this sense, I say to you in all sincerity, that faith in government is just another superstition – perhaps the greatest superstition of them all.

"Americans were among the very first of any nation to legally abolish slavery, and this fact should also never be forgotten. Nor should it ever be forgotten that this abolition of slavery was based *explicitly* upon and grounded thoroughly in principles and ideas born out of the Western Enlightenment. Americans were the first and the only people to as a nation identify and indict government for what it actually is: an apparatus of force. The overwhelming statist element required in order for slavery to persist is an element too often unacknowledged. Slavery cannot survive its legal repeal. Prior to America, for all human history, the entire world held to the opposite conviction: whether implicitly or explicitly, the world has always maintained that the natural state of humankind is a state in which government has legitimate primacy over the individual. This, the world has always believed, is in complete compliance with natural law, and one could even say that it was regarded as a sort of metaphysically determined fate. Citizens may, of course, disagree around the edges with this or that specific government policy or decree, and citizens may even rebel against it – yet only to replace it with a new state-ordered set of laws deemed 'more suitable' for humans to obey. The spirit which across the world make most people putty-like and therefore pliable, easy to mold and to rule, is still comparatively alien to Americans. It must be kept that way. It must at all costs be kept alien. Because human freedom is a birthright. In fact, it must be made *more* alien in the psyche of the people, the youth especially: you good people. This pundit thinks this should be legalized but not that, while this other pundit thinks that should be regulated but not this. This one believes (and will fight you to the death over the fact) that this amount of taxation is permissible in this specific arena of human activity, but not that amount in this particular arena. This other pundit thinks this sphere of human action should be regulated, but not that one, or that one (yet this one is okay). Another believes that this act should be decriminalized but not this other one. Listen to me, please: they *all* must be jettisoned and replaced with a sound principle: the principle of equal individual rights, which are purely negative liberties — specifying not what government should provide but rather what government and all other individuals must abstain from doing. This quibbling endlessly over details can get nowhere — except back where it all began: does each individual human being, regardless of race, sex, sexual-orientation, gender, color, class, or creed, possess the inalienable right to her own person and property — and only that — or does she not?

"Fundamentally, there only two types of societies

possible: those which are built upon individual freedom and its corollary: voluntary exchange. And those which consist of compulsion, coercion, violence, and force. There is no other kind of freedom besides the kind which voluntary exchange can bring about. When societies are mixed, as all societies including America have been, bad principles drive out good principles – *unless* the good principles are fully defined and philosophically systematized. Then and only then will the good drive out the bad. Ultimately what ushers in bad principles and ultimately what creates the mindsets that support bad principles and entrenches them, is, I truly believe, a sense of guilt – unearned guilt mixed with laziness in not questioning bad ideas – and that is precisely what today's so-called Critical Race Theorists, seemingly ignorant of the actual historical record of racism and slavery across all cultures on every single inhabited continent since the dawn of humankind, will stop at nothing to fully instill within Americans. And yet even in spite of their herculean effort, America has still retained its essential spirit: independence and liberty. *You must not let it die.* Whereas in every other place on planet earth besides America, service to state is still regarded as a duty – a duty and allegiance not ever to be questioned but simply obeyed – Americans have never felt any such sentiment, and that is a very good thing. Most Americans still admire achievement because most Americans still understand first-hand where achievement comes from, and what it takes to reach and hold."

She fell momentarily silent and sipped her water through the plastic straw I'd harpooned down through the ice.

"Earlier today," Katya Reyes said, "I was introduced to a middle-aged man – a visiting professor from Belarus who had never before been to America — and do you know what was the only thing he could talk to me about? He spoke to me over and over of his astonishment at how 'at ease' and 'enthusiastic' and 'happy' Americans of all walks of life are among each other. This man was only partly referring to the way bankers and Wall-Street types mingled and played darts and shot pool with the men who worked at the cement-plant or the road-construction fellows, or with the women who worked at the beauty salons and the bars. 'People aren't like that in Europe,' he said to me. 'People in America are easy-going, relaxed. Except for the academics,' he said, 'who seem angry and unhappy.'

"He's right. The culture of worn-out, crumbling, shabby Marxism worshipping at the shrine of misery and suffering and victimization – trying to convince the rest of the world that humans absent government-coercion are helpless, miserable, impotent creatures, incapable of human flourishing and helping their fellows voluntarily — it's pathetic and sickening. I told him that easiness and enthusiasm and happiness is the natural state when people are left alone and free. I told him also that the happiness which he saw in Americans outside of academia was the true spirit of America, and that America, for all her sins, for all her flaws, is the only place in human history to have discovered the secret, and to have striven to implement it.

"'What is the secret?' he asked me.

"The secret, I said to him, as I say to you, is in the very nature of what unleashes this easy-going happiness, this relaxed intermingling of people. It is the freedom of each individual to pursue her own life and happiness – and only her own life and happiness. It is the principle of individualism and individual rights which, even when breached, fundamentally defines America and which at all costs must never be lost. Because once it's gone, it cannot be gotten back.

"America is the only place ever to completely abolish, on a widespread and legally protected scale, the class-system and replace it with politico-ethical principles: the legal sanction for all humans – all colors, all sexes, all races, all walks of life – to strive for and become whatever their desire, ambition, and drive strives to achieve: to be self-made, as so many millions in America are and have become. It is not dog-eat-dog, as the propagandists never tire of describing it as, nor is it anti helping others or anti-charity. It is the very opposite: it generates the wealth that makes charity and helping others possible. Because America is still relatively free, the spectrum of wealth and achievement is still in America not fixed or static, as it is in a class or caste system, but can be moved along at any time, based chiefly upon individual desire, ambition, will. Luck plays only a minor role, no matter what the elites in academia have hammered into your head all these decades, and the statistics on this point are overwhelming. The legally guaranteed right to pursue life, liberty, and happiness does *not,* however, mean that you or I or anyone are guaranteed success or anything like it, but only that we all have the freedom to try, along with the legal guarantee (and this is crucial) that *if* you or I achieve it, it is ours inalienably. And this, my good young people, is why humans from all over the world have always flocked to America, and still do, even in spite of the horrifying erosion of her foundational principle."

She drained her rum, and I refilled it the moment she set her big snifter back down. She seemed for a split second surprised at the speed of my refill, but her grasshopper mind was quick to apprehend my desire to keep her socially lubricated. Oh, she was doing magnificently, I thought. She nodded almost imperceptibly at me and winked, rapidly.

"The progressive-academic left," she continued, "the so-called limousine liberals, they clamor for

Marxism and Neo-Marxism, and yet none of them have ever lived under any Marxist regime nor could ever survive it if they did – for one reason: because they'd be gunned-down instantaneously by Che Guevara or one of his many wannabees or any one of the Castros or their lackeys – and for what crime? The crime of protesting and speaking aloud? Yes, precisely that. And for their sexual preferences. For the private preferences and the very protests they are allowed in America without question or qualm — the America they loathe: for the right to free-speech to which they've grown so accustomed and by which they've been so spoiled that they now have the nerve to want to abolish it for the rest of humanity – and replace it with what? I will tell you: an elite bureau who deems for all of us what is 'allowable speech.'

"Yes," said the woman with the grasshopper mind to this small group at my bar on that memorable Tuesday evening, "you cannot quite crucify me for saying this, can you? Not as you would crucify your fellow Americans, at any rate, since I've lived under and survived two different regimes of socialism, and you have not. None of you. Since I'm a political refugee and know firsthand what bloodbaths these regimes are capable of creating and do routinely create, the oppression, the complete suppression of rights, which is an inherent feature of all forms of socialism, no matter the guise, no matter the trend, no matter the fad. Because I am not an American by birth but by preference, and so this automatically confers upon me an advantage which none among you have. So I will continue."

She sipped her refilled rum.

"These same sort of academic elites, in Europe as much as in America, would abolish and destroy the American soul in an instant, if they could, and are attempting to do just that – with great success, in certain circles, especially academia, with all the young vulnerable minds ready to be molded and shaped, and also by intentionally pushing for and passing more laws upon more laws, followed by more laws, which breed incremental dependence upon government, so that, before anybody quite knows how it happened, there is nothing but full-fledged helplessness and dependence and apathy in the minds of a majority — the minds of young people inculcated with the poisonous doctrine that human beings acting *voluntarily*, without the, quote-unquote, 'aid' (i.e. coercion) of government, can never flourish and solve societal problems. If you only hear one thing I'm saying to you now, let it be this:

"The greatest threat to any country's health and freedom is the incremental dependence and help-lessness that government controls foster and breed. More controls mean that more controls will be necessary — in the attempt to fix the problems that the original controls created in the first place. The controls thereby mushroom, propagate, never end. Controls beget more controls. It is a cycle which is interminable. Only the uncompromising implementation of principles to supplant them can stop it — by uprooting it completely.

"Do you know the most insidious part about this entire process? It is that once controls are in place, it is extraordinarily difficult, if not impossible, to remove them. And why? Because aided by the relentless propaganda machines, right, left, or middle — it doesn't matter at all — which push for and push through these controls to begin with, there is established in this process a kind of indoctrinated mind within the people, so that life with so many regulations and controls and arbitrary laws becomes completely normalized, the only thing people know, and human existence thus becomes unthinkable without these regulations and controls. It therefore becomes the only option in the minds of the people, the only way imaginable: a way of life. The independent mind, the thinking mind and critical faculty, once suspended, become hampered almost irreparably, thus making it inconceivable to most humans that humans could ever survive and flourish and prosper without a government who distributes and redistributes and provides all these things that they've become so dependent upon and accustomed to. Do you think I exaggerate? Look at how quickly this precise process of entrenchment took hold in the Soviet Union or China or Cuba, where once self-reliant people were made into total dependents and automatons in a matter of almost no time. The spirit of self-reliance was crushed so thoroughly, in so short a period, that it can really never be revived. Yes. *That* is what you must fight against. Fight it to the death, and do not cease fighting it, and do not let anyone convince you that you are cold-hearted or mean-spirited or anti-charity if you do not believe that helping others should be forced upon you or anyone at the point of a gun: a government gun. Forced charity is a contradiction in terms. Do not let the spirit of independence and freedom from government force be crushed out of existence.

"The thing that made America great and unique was not slavery — which was commonplace, every-where, and has always existed, before the Western Enlightenment ideas took hold — but rather the mindset and attitude diametrically opposite the insidious process I've just described: specifically, I mean, the implicit conviction most Americans had and still to some extent have that humans do *not* need government in order to prosper and act chari-tably — and always-always-always remember: the wealthier the country, the healthier the country. Government is in its best state a necessary evil and in its worst state an intolerable one, as Thomas Paine said, and as such government has one and only one legitimate function: to *protect* against the instigation of force, which includes jurisprudence and courts to adjudicate.

"The inanities of today – inanities at which most sane people now laugh – become the seriously taken shibboleths of tomorrow. This is an iron-clad truth which all of history bears out, and it is no small matter, my good people, and remember, please: those who can make you believe absurdities can also make you commit atrocities, if I may improvise a little upon Voltaire. Mr. Bartender, how's my hair?"

"Sleek and fair."

"Neither politics nor economics is primary," she said in closing, "but rather the consequential result of more fundamental philosophical ideas. The political-economic implementation of these ideas is always the final piece in a long and complex chain, and these idea-chains form the underpinnings of any given civilization. One cannot, therefore, fight or change the consequences without first fighting for the ideas that caused the consequences.

"A country is not some strange and sacrosanct thing that can't be dissected and defined. It is merely a large grouping of individual human beings, united by certain specified geographic borders and boundaries. The individuals who compose it must never be subordinated or subjugated to any tribe, group, or collective — no matter how purportedly necessary or admirable the cause.

"Upon the battleground of ideas, one does not need to win the majority. Please remember this. One does not need to convert everyone. History is made – and won – by intellectual ideas and ideological movements, which are in turn created not by majorities but small, splinter-like groups: groups composed of those individual people who are able and willing to take on the challenges of thought — who in so doing come to grasp and articulate the philosophical-intellectual issues of the day. Upon this battleground, it is not sheer numbers that matter most but rather the consistency and, even more, the quality of the ideas for which one is fighting, and how well they're understood — how thoroughly their principles are grasped.

"An intellectual movement does not start with organized action. Ideological tides do not begin with a campaign or an organization already fully in place. Philosophical battles are first, last, and always a battle for the human mind – specifically, I mean, the battle to demonstrate, through reason and logical proof, the truth or falsehood of ideas. In this sense, intellectual battles are philosophical battles, which are in turn battles of education: the battle to persuade one's fellows by elucidating the nature of the ideas being propounded and fought for. The logic and truth of the ideas being put forth – including the back-and-forth exchanges and counter-arguments – determine the degree of persuasiveness. It is for this reason that clearly defined, clearly articulated, thoroughly elaborated, and closely reasoned arguments are the most persuasive – because they are the right and true arguments: because humans have at their disposal only one method by which to demonstrate error, and that method is reason."

Katya Reyes stopped speaking here and immediately, in one large swallow, drained the last of her rum. She then set the big bulbous snifter down gently onto the bartop, placing a one-hundred dollar bill beneath the snifter's thin and crystal foot. "It's all yours, Mr. Bartender," said the woman with the strong and nimble mind, the grasshopper mind. "For your service to me and for the shots you devilishly over-measure."

"It was my pleasure."

THE ONE WHO SPENDS HER LIFE
EDUCATING HERSELF

MOST HUMANS DON'T THINK TOO much about the great problems of existence, concerning which, most behave as most around them behave.

Most people perform certain daily acts without paying particular attention to their acts, nor to the ideological theories or hierarchal structures under-girding them.

Most people do most things because most people became accustomed throughout childhood to doing most of these things. Most go through life holding views only passively acquired and only partially examined – views and convictions they grew up among, or perhaps, later, things they came to absorb from schoolmates and friends, which in turn came from various teachers and educators.

It remains a fact, however, that no matter the degree of societal inertia, we can always each *individ-*

ually (as long as the brain is healthy) educate ourselves and assume individual responsibility for the contents of our own minds.

"If you meet at dinner a man who has spent his life in educating himself — a rare type in our time, I admit, but still one occasionally to be met with — you rise from the table richer, and conscious that a high ideal has for a moment touched and sanctified your days," wrote Oscar Wilde.

It remains a fact also that the power which calls into human life and animates any social body is *always* ideological in its origins, and the very structure of homo-sapiens sapiens brain requires that humans live not by means of brute strength but by means of knowledge, which entails that we all, as humans, live by means of ideas.

It is for this reason a fundamental requirement of human life that we each on some level live by means of philosophy. This is true whether one is consciously aware of it or not, whether one likes it or not.

The ideological lethargy which characterizes most — though not all — humans and which funnels humans into an assembly-line-like process of passively or semi-passively accumulated philosophical ideas, is not, by any means, fated.

Independent thought, like intelligence itself, is a lifelong and continuous *process:* it is learned and cultivated.

Philosophy has three main branches, with three smaller branches growing from those first three. I list them below in their hierarchical order of importance:

Metaphysics: the study of independent reality (or existence).

Epistemology: the study of human knowledge.

Ethics: the study of human action.

Here are the three smaller branches, in order of their hierarchy:

Politics (a subdivision of ethics): the study of human action in groups.

Economics (a subdivision of politics): the study of production and exchange.

Esthetics (a subdivision of epistemology): the study of art.

(One can legitimately structure all subsequent branches as subdivisions of metaphysics, the most fundamental one, since metaphysics studies reality in total.)

These six branches are distinct and yet completely interwoven and continually growing, like branches grafted and forever grafting: interconnected, contextual.

Politico-economic policies are *always and only* the result — never the cause — of a long sequence of ethical and epistemological ideas, which are in turn the result of metaphysical ideas. Yet it is politico-economic policies which for each individual human being possesses the most destructive — or beneficial — potential.

Political power is the power to shape human action.

Since all human action is preceded by thought, the one who is politically powerful is so because her political strength and might is ultimately sourced in the power of ideas.

It is ideas only that can confer upon a person the enduring power to influence the choices and actions of others – enduring, I say, because one can become a lasting leader of other humans only if one is supported by ideas the acceptance of which makes other people willing to be led.

This point is of vital importance.

Power is thus *not* ultimately a physical thing but a moral-philosophical phenomena, which rests upon the subject's sanction: the sanction, specifically, of the ideology held by the one in power.

It is the distinguishing characteristic of the state to apply coercion, even to the point of imprisonment and violence (or its threat) against those who are neither willing to accept state-mandated decrees nor to act voluntarily in obeying them. Yet observe that even this physical oppression and violence, or its mere threat, is no less founded upon the power of ideas, insofar as she or he who advocates the application of violence needs the *voluntary* cooperation of at least some people, since a ruler can never rule by means of physical violence alone, but needs the ideological support of some group in order to subdue other groups – or, to put that another way:

> The despot must have a group of partisans who of their own accord obey the despot's dictates. This obedience and support is the thing that provides the despot with the necessary means by which she or he is able to rule others. Whether the despot's sway is long-lasting or short-lived depends entirely on the numerical relation of those who voluntarily support the despotism and those who do not.
>
> Though a tyrant may temporarily rule through a minority if this minority holds superior arms and methods of force over the majority, in the long run a minority cannot keep the majority in subservience. The oppressed will rise up in rebellion and cast off the yoke of tyranny. Any system of government that would endure must therefore construct itself upon a system of ideas accepted by the majority.

Wrote Ludwig von Mises.

(Present-day China — in the context of Hong-Kong particularly — provides a perfect illustration of this principle: because the Chinese military, including the police-force, remain *ideologically* aligned with the political regime in power, that regime is only thus able to continue its authoritarian rule. If, however, enough individual people *within* the military converted from the official Communist ideology and adopted a laissez-faire ideology — such as what Hong-Kong adopted when, for approximately one century, it was under British governance [and Sir John Cowperthwaite specifically] and flourished as no other place in human history excepting for early America — the regime in power could not maintain its position or last, but would be overthrown. This is why every authoritarian or even semi-authoritarian regime has a gigantic state-run propaganda apparatus: this apparatus is indispensable to their politic cabinet because it's vital in indoctrinating the citizenry, so that ideas and the flow of ideas can be controlled. This not only includes state-run media but also very strict censorship: no freedom of speech, no freedom of press, no freedom of media or anything like it, because these things would give ordinary people other ideas about what human life might also be like.)

Moral-ideological forces are the true forces that form the foundation of government and bequeath to rulers their *legal* power and sanction: the sanction and power to use force and violence against any renegade individuals or dissident minority-groups made up of such individuals.

It is for this precise reason also that the deterioration of the critical sense is among the most serious threats to true civilization – making it, in addition to everything else, horrifyingly simple for quacks and charlatans to fool people, which is in turn the reason you see people on either so-called side of the aisle now sincerely believe it when they're told that they can *only* be free if they relinquish their freedom – economic freedom first and foremost – in one form or another, whether it be in the name of "privilege," God, equality, "the environment," SARS-CoV2, or some other equally fallacious thing. The specifics are immaterial.

The logical elaboration of this ideology is that if people willingly cede their freedoms – putting more power into the hands of politicians and bureaucrats thereby, all of whom know better than we ourselves, as individuals, how best to conduct our lives and our affairs – we will, at last, finally contribute more fully and ably to that entity known as the "common good." The "common good" is in turn *not* specified by each individual voluntarily, since individuals are diverse and do not all possess the same values or ideas about what is good, but rather by the same politicians and bureaucrats to whom our freedoms have been ceded — and who, incidentally, will not hesitate to chop you or me off at the knees in exchange for money or votes.

Society, we're told, will only in this way become a better place.

It is my conviction that humans have at their

disposal one basic instrument with which to fight this or any other error, and that instrument is reason. This is why, I say, the only true independent thinker – the only true renegade or dissident – is the one who cultivates and uses the power of her reason.

Is there enough energy left in the American spirit and in the American people to save America and her quiddity, which is individuality, individualism, diversity, independence, freedom — the freedom to follow your dreams and to grow fabulously wealthy and to make of yourself what you will, shooting for the stars, provided only that you respect the equal freedom in others — a quiddity under the constant attack of intellectuals and academic elites and xenophobes who would subjugate you and me and everyone else in an instant, if they could, to a progressive bureau of planners which believes that humans are fundamentally defined and united *not* by their capacity to reason and think and choose and act cooperatively, voluntarily, but rather by their skin color, their genes, their gender, their sex, their sexual-orientation, their "minority status" or some other unchosen and equally non-definitional human characteristic, which, however, can only in the end (precisely *because* it is non-definitional) divide humans – divide and subdivide them – endlessly, and which in the process makes humans slaves to both their unchosen biochemical pedigree and also to the elite bureau whom they, the elites, have put in charge of the rest of us?

Is there?

It is impossible to say here for certain.

But those of us who do believe, with all our heart and soul, in the inviolate sanctity of each and every single individual's inalienable right to her own life and labor (property, never forget, is an extension of work and person) must stand up for Lady Liberty, her essence, wherever she exists — stand up and fight relentlessly, forcefully, philosophically, intellectually for her. We must stand up for her and at the same time stand *against* the constantly mutating forces of collectivism, primitivism, tribalism, and all the other ideas and ideologies that give rise to anti-individualism — deadly ideas which are the antithesis of what Lady Liberty represents:

We are each individuated and sovereign, endowed with the human faculty of volition, which is choice. And that is why we are sovereign: because we each possess volition.

I appeal to you to stand up for freedom and do not be cowed, bullied, or gainsaid in your belief of individualism and individuality — the equal rights of each and every individual human.

The good news is this: the ideas that ground all arguments *opposed* to individuality consist purely of smoke and mirrors: a theory of knowledge which purports to *know* that no knowledge is possible, a theory of existence which claims to know for certain (and for real) that reality is unreal and therefore unknowable, a politico-economic code which claims, despite the fact that knowledge is impossible, to *know* better than we ourselves, as individual human beings, what's best for all of us — the "collective" — how we must collectively live our lives because, at the bottom of it, we're told, individuals don't even really exist, and so this ethical code will by necessity be implemented by force, for the common good of all, of course. Of course.

Such an ideology is not intellectually difficult to vanquish. But to give and support a full and forceful philosophical refutation of these antithetical ideas, it is necessary to refute the ideological principles *beneath* them, and it takes time and constant effort. Defending the principles of human individuation, even if the defense is impregnable, isn't sufficient. The offensive must be taken.

So I say again: don't be bullied or shamed for believing in your individuality and the power of your volition, your independent brain, and your ability to think — to think for yourself — and to choose your own values and live your own life as *you,* an individuated human being and not some cog in a non-existent collective, wish to live it: to cooperate with your fellow human beings not by coercion but voluntarily, peacefully, in a mutually advantageous and pleasant way for all the individual human beings involved. All you need to do is stand up for that *principle* and do not allow anyone to bully you or bribe you out of it.

In order to vanquish irrationalism and the authoritarian command-and-control it requires, humans must, I repeat, take the offensive — not merely battling *against* irrationalism, but also in support *of* the supremacy of independence and individual autonomy and independent thought, which things ground in fact the inalienable right of each and every individual, person and property alike, regardless of race, sex, sexual-orientation, color, class, creed, or gender. Human individuation and the faculty of volition are what ground individual rights in fact. Individual rights, in turn, legally guarantee each individual the liberty to exist without the permission of the state or municipality, which state or municipality exists *only* to serve each individual, to *protect* her right to life and property, and not the other way around.

In standing up in support and full sanction *of* this, you will obliterate all the pseudo-intellectual arguments that have infected the world with a constantly mutating ideological disease, killing, in the process, and enslaving and imprisoning countless billions of individual human lives — individual human lives like yours and mine.

Because the truth is that the ideas underpinning all anti-individual, anti-freedom irrationalism and collectivism are so bloody weak that when you get past the maze of Kafka-traps and the mine-fields of equivocation and circumlocution and the gauntlet of other fallacies, the ideas confronting you wither away and melt into nothingness. It is, make no mistake, an intellectual battle and the battlefield is long and tilted, with a large army, craven to the core but anonymous and safe in their homes and so hair-trigger-ready to cyber-harass and cyber-cancel you, but I ask you this in all seriousness:

What more than each and every individual's independence and autonomy – all humans equal in individual rights: equal in rights before the law, all sizes, sexes, orientations, genders, all eye colors and skin colors – what, I ask, could be a more glorious purpose or plight for which to battle and to fight?

A LIQUID LIFE, FOREVER FLOWING

THE ART of independent thinking is the art of individual inquiry, and individual inquiry is rooted in observation.

When a child learns through personal experience, by bouncing it on a concrete surface, that a properly filled basketball can be dribbled, but then after testing the same basketball on a different sort of surface (lush grass or the liquid surface of a swimming pool or perhaps a muddy road), or upon attempting to bounce the same ball on the same concrete court though this time when the basketball is not properly filled with air — her new observations and this new information do *not* falsify the things she's already discovered and learned about dribbling a properly filled basketball on a concrete court.

Rather, her new observations *expand* her knowledge. They add information which she then integrates into her preexisting information, enlarging her context thereby. This new information, she then synthesizes or blends with data she's already stored inside her mind, broadening the scope of her knowledge by broadening her context.

All knowledge is contextual.

Learning is largely a process of context expansion.

In this way, the scope of the child's learning grows as her context grows. The exact same process is at work when she experiments with a leather basketball, versus a rubber or vinyl basketball, on a wooden court, versus an asphalt or a clay court.

Through direct observation and experience — and not upon faith or upon another's say-so — the child learns where and how to dribble.

Later, through this same basic process, she perhaps learns why.

New knowledge, if it's accurately observed — which is to say, if it's true ("true" meaning "accurate") — does not falsify the previously known. It elaborates it by elaborating the context. It would be difficult to overstate the importance of this principle.

The independent thinker does not keep an "open mind" with regard to all questions — if, that is, an "open mind" means she does not come to definite conclusions or form definite convictions about things she's observed, or about the new things she will observe. Nor does she keep a "closed mind," believing that no actual knowledge can ever be gotten because contexts always change, and because observations, like memories, are irremediably flawed, anyway, since the senses are not nor can ever be considered reliable. These are popular fallacies, and we would all do well to look a little suspiciously upon the open-minded-close-minded concepts.

What, then, in the final analysis, determines if knowledge is actual and reliable?

The results in reality.

The results in reality are the full and final measure by which all knowledge is evaluated and gauged. Does the ball bounce? Does the structure stand? Does the wheel roll without breaking? Does the vehicle get us from point A to point B? Does the matchstick spark a fire? Does the hunter get her prey? Does the Space Shuttle fly into orbit? Does the liquid properly pour when the strainer is placed over the mixing glass? Does whiskey lose its potency when it's heated to a boil? Does the vessel float even when loaded with heavy cargo?

If truth is the accurate identification of reality — and it is — then knowledge equals truth.

Thus the independent mind is neither the "open mind" nor the "closed mind" but the inquisitive, vigorous mind: it is a critical-thinking mind, one for whom little is self-evident, except ultimately the material provided by the senses from which, beginning at birth or even before, all subsequent learning flows and is, at least in theory, continually growing — and please, reader, never doubt this: it is a liquid life, forever flowing.

A fundamental or foundational fact is a fact which cannot be broken down into smaller parts or pieces, nor be derived from previous facts.

Why can't it?

Precisely *because* it's fundamental.

It's fundamental and therefore "axiomatic" — which means that any attempt to refute these fundamental facts must nevertheless rely upon and use these very same facts, even in the most succinct or clever attempts to refute them. They are inescapable in the literal sense. (The attempt to prove that proof is invalid is an example of this: "proof" by definition means the preponderance of evidence which admits no alternative. Any attempt to prove that this is invalid requires the very thing you're trying to invalidate: a preponderance of evidence.)

There are phenomena which cannot be analyzed and traced back to other phenomena. They are the ultimate given. The progress of scientific research may succeed in demonstrating that something previously considered as an ultimate given can be reduced to components. But there will always be some irreducible and unanalyzable phenomena, some ultimate given.

Wrote Ludwig von Mises.

The independent thinker is the thinker who takes responsibility for the content of her own mind.

The art of independent thought is, I'll say it again (and again), the art of individual inquiry, and individual inquiry is rooted in observation, which includes introspection. The realities of the soul, though intangible, are realities nonetheless.

Incontrovertibly, the independent thinker depends, like everybody, upon the knowledge of experts and specialists, whether medical, legal, mechanical, scientific, or anything else, and yet the thing that separates the independent thinker from the passive thinker is this:

The independent thinker is always willing to reinvestigate theories generally accepted or deemed true — to retrace, if need be, and to follow every idea down to its foundation, its irreducible fundamental.

The willingness and even the insistence to reinvestigate theories decreed as true — especially when matters of life and personal freedom are at issue — is the one and only legitimate meaning of the term "open-mind."

If any theory or ideology contradicts a fundamental fact, it is false.

Human freedom is fundamental. It is grounded in the human quiddity: the rational faculty, which can operate fully and optimally only when left free, and the results of which when it is unshackled and untrammeled are human flourishing.

The error many make when thinking about questions that are ultimately philosophical is the tendency to accept outcomes and results — i.e. ends — while at the same time not paying attention to or understanding the causes: to take as a given the end result of a long sequence of thought or chain of reasoning, or to regard it as a self-evidency, while neither paying attention to nor grasping all that's presupposed in this process.

It is a serious error to regard ideological contradictions as harmless or even, as is often the case, healthy, beneficial, or good.

Ideological contradictions and inconsistencies may, at times, be masked by adding to an already faulty sequence of reasoning — thus postponing the emergence of a manifest conflict — but they will also, in this process, exacerbate the bad things that they mask, and in so doing, they will render any true and final solution much more difficult to obtain. They compound the agonies and amplify the hatreds — making peaceful, cooperative settlements impossible. They increase vitriol and violence. Unfortunately, the vast majority of politico-economic ideologies accepted by public opinion — worldwide

— are infected down to their core with contradictions and inconsistencies: contradictions and inconsistencies caused by the volitional nature of the human mind, which because of its volitional nature render it fallible, subject to errors.

We are all fallible. We all make errors, all of us, all the time. Correcting them (or not) is what separates the wheat from the chaff, the baby from the bath, the serpent from the staff.

Errors uncorrected are the root cause of ideological infection.

These infections consist mostly of an eclectic collocation of ideas incompatible with one another and the contents of which, therefore, because they're incompatible, cannot withstand logical scrutiny. Their inconsistencies are irreparable and as such defy any attempts to integrate their various parts into a system of ideas compatible with one another.

Some try to justify the contradictions within their accepted ideologies by attempting to name the supposed advantages of compromising among them all — so that a more "dynamic" view of human relations can develop: "a more dynamic and smoother functioning of inter-human relations," as it has been described to me. Frequently, these same people fall back upon the common fallacy that life and reality are "not logical or reasonable," and they will often also maintain that a contradictory system will prove its "dynamic expediency and worth" and even its truth by "working satisfactorily," whereas a logically consistent ideological system would, they say, result in disaster.

There is no need now to rebut these popular errors — insofar as these popular errors at all times rebut themselves.

Reason does not follow some separate sluice from real life. Reason and real life are symmetrical and harmonious. They follow the same sluice. Reason is human consciousness, which is the human faculty of awareness. Real life is existence, which is that which exists: that *of* which awareness is aware. Contradictions cannot exist in reality, apart from human consciousness, because reality is as it must be: perfectly symmetrical and harmonious. For homo-sapiens, reason is the only means by which to grasp and master the problems of reality. What is contradictory in theory constitutes an error — an error in the attempted apprehension of real life as it actually is — and for this reason, ideological inconsistencies, which should be corrected, cannot provide satisfactory, working solutions for the problems offered by the facts of the world and the universe, including the universe within each. The only thing that can result from holding contradictory ideologies is the concealment of the real problems and thus the prevention of finding in time solutions which are sound and satisfying.

THE BROWN-EYED BEAUTY OF DISTILLED SPIRITS

BRANDY IS the brown-eyed beauty of distilled spirits — the one from whom you can never *quite* get away, despite her flawed and fugitive nature.

What I like most about brandy is what I like most about people: her almost inexhaustible versatility.

Brandy is a distilled spirit made from fermented fruit juice.

Most often, the fruit juice comes from grapes, and this is why you'll frequently hear brandy described as a spirit made with distilled wine, which is not entirely accurate. I include brandy in a book titled *Whiskey Wisdom* because whiskey owes something of its heritage to brandy.

Joe Heron, founder of a brandy distillery called Copper & Kings, in Louisville, Kentucky, describes it this way:

"Distilled from grapes or other fermented fruit

and often aged in oak casks, brandy is to grapes as whiskey is to grain — the distilled essence of its materials, aged to enhance flavor, blended for balance, then sipped or mixed."

The Dutch didn't invent brandy, but the name comes from a Dutch word: *brandewijn* — or brandy-wine — which means "burnt wine."

It should also be reiterated that not all brandy comes from grapes but can be made from any fruit or fruits — apples, for instance, or pears, or apricots, or cherries, or virtually any other fruit as well.

It's not precisely known when in human history people discovered that we can convert food into alcohol through the process of fermentation. It is ancient. A strong argument can be made that the first distilled spirits were horse-milk brandies, whose alcohol was separated not through heat distillation but through cold distillation — which is to say, by freezing water out of the fermented horse milk during those long Mongolian winters.

Brandy, understand, is the genus under which many, many species are subsumed.

The French call fruit-based brandies *eau-de-vie* (pronounced: oh-du-VEE), which means "waters of life" (as, incidentally, do the words "whiskey" and "whisky" and "aquavit" and "vodka").

Most brandy, like most whiskey, is aged in barrels, the wood from which imparts a great deal of character and color and flavor to the brandy. You are perhaps familiar with the terms V.S. (for Very Special) and V.S.O.P. (Very Special Old Pale) and X.O (for Extra Old). These are labeling terms that refer to the length of time the brandies have been aged.

Distilling brandy is a bastard art, very seductive to some, but make no mistake: she can break your heart.

WHISKY, WHISKEY, WHITE-LIGHTNING, MOONRAKER, MOONSHINE

THE OLDEST WRITTEN record of the distillation process — and that process refers specifically to a process of separating the components of any given liquid-mixture by using some combination of boiling and condensation — comes to us from approximately 100 AD, when an ancient Greek philosopher named Alexander ("Alexander of Aphrodisias," as he's known) described the act of taking sea water and distilling it into pure drinking water.

The first known origins of whiskey distillation began over one-thousand years ago, when distillation made the migration from mainland Europe into Scotland and Ireland, almost certainly by way of traveling monks.

The Scottish and Irish monasteries did not have the vineyards and grapes of Europe, you see, and so these monks instead turned to fermenting grain mash. This resulted in what's now thought to be the first distillations of modern whiskey.

The first written record of the word we now know as *whiskey* (or *whisky*, if you prefer, the difference being purely what country you're from: Ireland and America spelling it *whiskey*, Scotland, Canada, and pretty much the rest of the world spelling it *whisky*) appears in 1405 — in The Irish Annals of Clonmacnoise — where it was written that the head of a certain clan "died after taking a surfeit of aqua-vitae during the Christmas season."

The differences in spelling are, I repeat, superficial and regional and come from the differences in translations of the word *uisge-beatha* — meaning "water of life" — from the Scottish and Irish Gaelic forms.

The Old Bushmills Distillery, licensed in Northern Ireland, holds the title of oldest licensed whiskey distillery in the world — dating clear back to 1608.

WHITE-LIGHTNING, Moonraker, Moonshine

If it shed any light on the subject at all — and it doesn't even begin to — I might, for whatever it's worth, be tempted to elaborate on the actual term "moonshine," and where it originated: i.e. rural England (circa 1780), when country smugglers hid illicit barrels of French *brandy* (note that) in shallow ponds in order to avoid the taxman. But they were discovered one fated summer night, when the moon shone so brightly upon the surface of the pond that it looked as though a wheel of cheese were floating in the water. And so these bootleggers told the taxmen that they were raking the water *not* for contraband but for a creamy piece of the cheese they saw shimmering therein.

But this is all rumor and rodomontade, easily sliced with an investigative blade.

It is, though, universally agreed that the term "moonshine" does indeed come from the term "moonraker," which in turn comes from that legend.

It is also generally agreed that moonshine, the actual alcohol — or white-lightning, if you prefer, or white-whiskey, or mountain dew, all of which are regional names for moonshine — entered America in the early 1800's, when Scots-Irish immigrants, who back home often made their whiskey without aging it (which is essentially vodka, by the way — which, like the word "whiskey," means "water-of-life"), began settling the Appalachian region of America.

Still, the question remains — a question the answer to which is not straightforward or easy to track down: if many vodkas are essentially white whiskies, and if many whiskies made of corn mash are *not* moonshine, what, in the final analysis, is the thing that defines moonshine?

The answer, it turns out, is this:

Legality versus illegality.

Moonshine, notorious for its high proof — frequently hovering around 190 (yowza!) — is *any* distilled spirit concocted in an unlicensed still. That is the definition.

This includes so-called splo, or bathtub gin, or the harrowing hooch cooked-up by your next-of-kin.

This is a little-known yet wonderful whiskey cocktail, which can be made with rye or bourbon, up or on-the-rocks. It's also excellent when made with scotch.

WORK

It's not merely for money that healthy humans work. Before free-exchange which created specialization which created the division of labor, the vast majority of human exertion was directed toward one thing and one thing only, and that was the production of food.

For most of human history, people labored their entire lives, from sun-up to sundown, six or seven days a week, and they did so just to survive. For many centuries and millennia, life was, as Thomas Hobbes so memorably described it, "nasty, brutish, and short."

Free-exchange changed all of that.

Free-exchange created specialization which created the division of labor, which unleashed human ingenuity and human productivity.

Consider, for a moment, what your shoes and

your clothes would look like now if you had to find the time to make and stitch and skin and tan and sew all the material yourself — in between the never-ending labor of producing or catching or gathering your food.

Consider what our transportation would look like if it was up to each of us to come up with our own means of it — whether horse, camel, boat, wheel, or airplane.

Consider how much would be required for each to produce the fuel *alone* for an automobile or airplane.

Consider medicine, including care for broken bones, strep throat, appendix bursting, gallbladders, abscessing teeth, birth control.

Now consider how we have all this and so much more at our very fingertips.

The reason we have such quick and easy access to all this is a reason so basic that most people don't fully see or grasp it: free-exchange and the division of labor.

Because of free-exchange, we can trade with others who have things that we ourselves want and cannot do or do not *want* to do — be it all manner of food production, shelter, clothing, medicine, transportation, light, entertainment, and much much more.

This process is the essence of economics and economic growth.

Because of specialization, more and more people are doing what they *want* to do, and not what they *must* do for bare subsistence.

Because of specialization, our work has now increasingly become an expression of who we are, what we love and become good at — an expression and an emphasis of it — and this is one reason that work has become such a fundamental component to human happiness: it expresses our efficacy as we keep doing it — practicing it, in essence — becoming better and better. Work gives direction and expression to the movements of our bodies as dictated by our brains.

Work — all work — is our person and personality concretized in human action and human motion.

Work gives physical form-and-shape to our psychological existence.

In fostering and developing a sense of self-efficacy and productiveness, work also, as a corollary — a necessary by-product, you could even say — develops a sense of self-worth.

This life-affirming truth about work is one of the countless things which power-lusting politicians, in their reckless, impulsive, uninformed responses to crises and their push to establish dependency among voters, have completely missed:

Successfully panicking the majority over something that makes sick only a fractional portion of the population and kills far less, the same voter-obsessed politicians expressed their panic by means of the only method at their disposal: force. The forced shutdown of economic activity.

If you remember nothing else, I ask you in all sincerity to remember this:

Government is *by definition* an agency of force.

Thus, terrified by something beyond their powers of comprehension, government agents substituted their myopic, minuscule knowledge for that of an incomprehensibly vast marketplace — putting millions and millions and millions of human beings instantaneously out of work thereby and exploding millions and millions and millions of businesses into which people had invested their entire lives.

Having enacted *overnight* an economic collapse that wiped out the livelihoods of tens of millions of human beings, these same politicians then proceeded doubling down and then tripling down in their reckless panic: acting still in blind-panic and uncertainty, extracting trillions of dollars from the private economy, and accordingly they began throwing money indiscriminately at a problem largely of their own devising.

Let us also note and let us never forget: politicians were only able to do this (albeit temporarily) thanks entirely to the economic growth that has nothing to do with politicians and absolutely everything to do with people becoming passionate about their work.

No matter what your political convictions — no matter how far to the left or no matter how far to the right or no matter where in the middle, no matter the political-moral ideologies you've grown up among or learned in school or anything else, no matter what you've come to believe and accept, whether implicitly or explicitly — I ask you to consider that last thing deeply:

The *only* reason *any* government can spend *any* money on *any* problem in *any* realm of human activity is this: the economic growth created and produced **not** by politicians and their bureaus but by people who care about their work.

HUMAN ABILITY IS ROOTED in the human brain. What we as individuals ultimately become grows out of this root, and nothing more fundamental than work is required for the life we want for ourselves.

No matter what moral code anyone tries to force upon you, whether secular or non-secular, the true measure of value is found in our work: in our effort and passion for learning and striving and becoming better.

The truth is that only a small minority of the world's population understands firsthand how jobs are created, how income is generated, how payrolls are met. Economies are living, breathing organisms of infinite complexity. The majority of the world's population thinks wages and wealth appear more or less magically. If businesses are shutdown for our own good, therefore, surely those business-owners will simply wave their magic wand to conjure their magic wealth in order to start up those magical businesses all over again, when, at last, this panic has ended.

The fact that business-owners and entrepreneurs have been sacrificed in such an appalling manner is of no real importance to elected politicians. I believe that most people know, at least implicitly, that this is how politicians operate. The real crime and the most terrifying and dangerous thing of all is that most non-politicians (i.e. voters) *also* now do not care about this colossal destruction.

> It is only a government that can count on the support of the governed which can establish a lasting regime. Whoever wants to see the world governed according to his own ideas must therefore strive for domination over human minds. It is impossible, in the long run, to subject people against their will to a regime that they reject.

Wrote economist Ludwig von Mises.
Politicians have made it clear that a certain type

of worker cannot in their eyes be trusted, just as certain types of businesses can't be trusted, to remain open during a time of crisis. Their message was that they'd lock us down for our own good — and yet try to pay us off by means of the economy they'd simultaneously shut down, while we were *at the same time* forced by governmental decree to remain idle.

How these out-of-touch these elitists are. How completely they miss the entire point:

Precisely *because* so many working-people love doing the work they do and have become good at it, these selfsame workers would have made all manner of changes to their daily routines so that they could continue to work.

How can I be so sure?

Precisely because free workers already had made all manner of adjustments in their working habits, so that they could do what makes them shine — what makes them happy — and they began doing it *voluntarily*, before the exertion of state force made it illegal to do anything otherwise.

In his book *32 Yolks*, Chef Eric Ripert described the star-like "charisma that comes from those who are truly good at what they do."

Every politician and bureaucrat on the planet should read this book. It doesn't matter at all that the overwhelming majority of them wouldn't under-stand the truths expressed therein about the nature of work and the joy and passion and self-worth that humans beings derive from their work — the importance of competency and skill, how the meaning of life can be found precisely there, in purposeful action, the motions of the human body in concert with the human brain — it doesn't matter at all, I say, because, just possibly, for one out of a thousand of these bureaucrats, it *might* spark a little light inside the mind. And that is enough: because for this one-in-a-thousand few, they might then begin to grasp why work is *so* much more than merely a way to pay the bills:

Work is the physical expression of our thoughts.

Work gives shape to our minds.

Work is the literal extension of our selves — our very person.

Work is the flesh to our spirit, the body to our brains.

EQUALITY IS UNFAIR AND
INTRINSICALLY UNJUST

SINCE HUMANS ARE each individuated beings, with a singular consciousness, born into a complex system of nature, humans are because of this infinitely diverse. This is a good thing, and it is a beautiful thing. This infinite diversity means, however, that humans are inherently unequal – in countless different ways.

There is absolutely nothing wrong with this.

Diversity means inequality.

"The diversity of humankind is a basic postulate of our knowledge of human beings [and so] it can be shown that equality of income is an impossible goal for humankind," wrote the economist George Reisman.

It is a fallacy to think that equal is or ever should be regarded as a moral virtue. But quite apart from the moral aspect of it, there's this as well: it is from a purely practical standpoint impossible to achieve even *approximate* equality among human beings – though one of the most shocking and horrifying attempts is Pol Pot's Cambodia and the Khmer Rouge (the name of his communist regime), which by some estimates massacred a *quarter* of Cambodia's entire population in the attempt to reach an egalitarian society.

In the sphere of human activity, there is only one legitimate meaning of the word "equality," and that is *not* "equality of opportunity," as you hear so many on both so-called sides of the aisle say. It is equality before the law – or "equal in rights," as it has been well-described by certain philosophers of the law. Equality before the law – or equality of individual rights – means full and total recognition of the individual's inalienable right to life and property, regardless of the individual's race, sex, sexual-orientation, color, class, gender, beauty, brains, or brawn: inalienable rights, as the very word *inalienable* denotes, are rights fully recognized, specified, sanctioned, and protected by law, among *all* individual humans equally.

Quoting Hebert Spencer, according to whom, in his excellent essay "Law of Equal Freedom" (from his book *Social Statistics*), "Every human has freedom to do all he or she wills, provided one infringes not the equal freedom of any other person. The freedom of each must be bounded by the similar freedom of all.... [And] every person may claim the fullest liberty to exercise his or her faculties compatible with the possession of like liberty by every other person."

This idea (which is a colossal intellectual achievement that took centuries to develop) owes a great deal to the post-Renaissance interest in the Ancient Greek philosophies of Stoicism and Epicureanism, both of which, working from the iron-firm foundation that all human beings possess the faculty of reason, maintained that each individual therefore must possess the "equal ability" to pursue a happy and virtuous life. (Happiness is not and cannot be guaranteed.) Epicurus and his followers were early proponents of the (still) radical idea of what is now often termed a "social contract," which means a legally protected "sphere of autonomy" wherein every individual has self-interested reasons to respect the equal rights of every other individual. This idea, it is surmised by some (myself included), influenced later codifications of the Roman concept of *jus* (as in "justice"), which in many ways became the basis of Ancient Roman law, whose influence on modern legal systems has been almost incalculably immense: several legal systems of the world (including the current civil law system of Europe) were "shaped significantly by the concepts of Roman law" (source).

Inequality, I say again, is an inherent feature of existence, but more than that: inequality is an inherent feature of freedom, and it is a good and healthy thing. It means diversity — a celebration of diversity and the freedom to pursue individual happiness and the life you wish for yourself and your loved ones, which is not uniformly the same for all human beings, since we are each individuated, possessing innumerable different values, and not mindless, Borg-like automatons.

It has never been my goal or desire to be a billionaire. But maybe it's yours. We should each *by right* be free to *pursue* the lives we want for ourselves, bounded only by the legally protected equal right and freedom of others. If we achieve all or even only a part of what we're pursuing, it is ours inalienably.

When humans are left alone, humans naturally stratify.

Why so, precisely?

Because humans possess varying degrees of "energy, ambition, and persistence," in the words of researcher Dr. Dean Simonton, of University of California, Davis, who studies genius, creativity, and eccentricity. These attributes are without question the greatest factors in determining achievement.

"Ambition," Dr. Simonton also says, "is energy and desire."

These attributes can be cultivated, fostered, developed, grown — because they remain within one's control. I do not say that there aren't possible factors of environment and genetics which may influence them; yet, even so, they *still* fall squarely within the realm of volition — primarily because they are rooted in the most fundamental choice there is: the choice to pay attention, or not.

"Energy level may in some measure be genetic," Dr. Simonton says. "But a lot of the time it's more just finding the right thing to be energetic and ambitious about."

The bartender and the miner, the server and the statesman, the electrician and the banker, the litigator and the soda jerk, the real-estate agent and the truckdriver, the baker and the beautician, the clerk and the custodian – they and everyone else, even humans within the same occupation, are "unequal" in a multitude of different ways, too many to ever quantify or calculate. Who could possibly be judge and jury over all this diversity and activity, and who would presume to determine which is superior and which lesser? Who?

There is nothing in nature – neither human nature nor nature apart from humans – which gives anyone legitimate authority over any other individual human being, person or property. Nothing. Do you feel me?

Do you see?

It is exactly for this reason that egalitarianism, as the term is commonly used in a poltico-economic context (i.e. "distributive justice," as it's sometimes now called by its adherents, or "entitlement theory," or "welfare economics") represents a monstrous injustice and violation of rights, since in order to equalize people, you must expropriate from others, whether they concede to it or not, so that you can "level the playing field" and "even-out the starting line," or "level the training field."

Please note that among adherents of egalitarianism and "distributive justice," it is a conclusion categorically forgone that voluntary human action — which is to say, giving each individual the choice to help level the playing field and even-out the starting line — is not nearly sufficient for these adherents, because the control they seek cannot be gotten through voluntary human action. This one fact alone — the necessity of compulsion and force — should tell you everything you need to know about the ideology.

There exists, as well, a foolproof method for demonstrating the colossal fallacy of egalitarianism as a political-economic philosophy, and that is in asking this question: by what natural law or by what edict, right, or rule-of-nature do you or anyone derive the authority to take by force, without consent, coercively, the justly gotten gains of one person so that you can redistribute it and give it to others?

In the history of the entire world, no good answer to that question has ever been given, and do you know why? Because no good answer for it exists.

The obsession with wealth-inequality is, I do sincerely believe, solely responsible for the staggering amounts of misinformation that exists on this topic. I am, of course, fully aware that tomes have been written which are diametrically opposed to my thesis here – some of these tomes even penned by Nobel-Prize winners in economics; others by thoroughly mediocre economists like Thomas Piketty – all of which resoundingly hammering the apocalyptic clarion over the "growing gap" between "rich and the poor," how "dangerous" it's become, and only growing more dangerous by the moment

I, who am no economist, could myself write volumes refuting every single one of these claims, and perhaps I will – though, for the record, it has already been done by many, many, many different people, including Nobel-Prize winning economists, who disagree with the wild-eyed rage and ideologies, the dogmatic theories advanced by these egalitarian true-believers.

(See also the compilation book *The Anti-Piketty.*)

But the truth is that you don't need to wade through all that dry technical economic data and discourse – and do you know why you do not need to?

Because the data is all around you, everywhere, and it is positively overwhelming.

Two-hundred-twenty years ago and for all of history before that, the entire world was poor – so poor, in fact, that even the wealthiest people in the world did not have access to the clean food, clean water, shelter, clothing, transportation, lumen hours, entertainment, and much, much, much, much, much more that even the poorest people in the developed world today now have instant access to.

Yes, you read that right, and it is incontrovertibly true.

Two-hundred-twenty years ago, the whole world was poor. Now, thanks *entirely* to the innovations which political-economic freedom unleashed, approximately two-hundred-ten years ago, less than ten percent of the world exists now in true poverty. And more than that: the wealthier the world grows, the more that true poverty *shrinks.*

Wealth begets wealth.

I furthermore madly want you to know and remember something else — a principle the importance of which simply cannot be overstated, and that principle is this: As long as any society remains poor, the *means* of dealing with societal issues remain proportionately poor. This is why wealthier countries are healthier countries: they are cleaner countries less environmentally degraded.

Poor countries are more polluted (by far), are dirtier and more environmentally degraded than wealthier countries. By far.

Wealth brings cleanliness.

Freedom fosters wealth.

The obsession with wealth inequality is, I am prepared to argue, the defining characteristics of virtually all progressive-leftist ideology, as it has been since the industrial revolution, when politico-economic freedom brought about greater specialization (the division of labor), which in turn brought about greater wealth and thus began increasing wealth inequality at last. Prior to industrialization, "egalitarianism" was the norm — and life was, as Thomas Hobbes famously described it, "nasty, brutish, and short." Do you know why?

Because the natural condition of humankind is extreme poverty and insecurity, and it is nothing more than romanticized nonsense to lament the passing of these happy days, these bucolic, agrarian, egalitarian days of primitive humans, when teeth rotted by age twenty (if you were lucky), when one out of three children died at birth (often taken the mother with them), when strep throat or dysentery killed you and life expectancies were mid-to-late thirties — when, in short, human life was basic barbarism at best.

This wealth-inequality obsession is, I am here to tell you all, a colossal waste of time and energy, totally misbegotten. "The defining challenge of our time," Obama described it as. He is wrong.

According to this anti-progress mentality, inequality is *the* primary problem of the modern world. It therefore demands a centralized solution. Thus, the oxymoronically named "progressives" — or the social democrats or the socialists (and the terminology here is inconsequential and irrelevant, purely a question of form and degree) – they push to use the power of the state in order to force the transfer of wealth from the financially productive and successful to those who are less so. This, they contend, is the right way to achieve "social justice."

Their error is rooted in their very premise. In addition to which, justice is an absolute and takes no qualifier. To give it a qualifier is to nullify its meaning.

Contrary to what this ideology would have you believe, the way to generate wealth is not to "exploit" customers, or workers. It is the opposite. Wealth is created by identifying certain problems or issues or desires which people have, and then coming up with and creating a product or service or solution which fulfills or satisfies their desire or solves their issue – enough so that they'll pay money for it.

It is critical to note that in this process, the consumer is the king and leader. I ask all readers to please never lose sight of this fact. The consumer leads the process by expressing her or his own preferences in the marketplace. Always. If a consumer feels that a product is overpriced, she or he will make no exchange. If a product seems worthwhile, the consumer will buy it willingly. It is a voluntary transaction in which *both* people gain and prosper. The sum of these individual choices — to purchase or not — make or break a business on the market, and this is the consumers' prerogative. In order to meet her or his own needs or wants, an individual must produce something or provide a service that satisfies another's needs or wants, whether they be rooted in labor, machinery, some sort of service, or a fine pair of pointy cowboy boots.

The consumer is free to purchase or good or service, or not. As long as the instigation of force is barred from human activity — as it should be — the power of choice remains entirely within the consumer.

Quoting the economist Antonis Giannakopoulos:

One of the socialists' key assumptions is that there is always a losing side in a transaction. They think that wealth is like a pie, and that the rich take the largest slice, leaving workers and customers with almost nothing. In reality the market is always expanding the pie, and voluntary exchanges are always win-win when they are made.

Bill Gates, Jeff Bezos, and all the other "evil capitalists" have managed to create an unprecedented amount of wealth, but not only for themselves. Those working for them have benefited from their jobs, and the people who buy their products and services have benefited from better or cheaper goods (or both). Other benefits include more time to pursue more important things, and in ways that cannot be quantified (i.e. they are measured in psychological profit). The entrepreneurs, in turn, have benefited from the services of their workers—which are well worth paying for. Entrepreneurs also benefit from the voluntary purchases made by their customers.

The huge fallacy among virtually all progressive-economic thinkers is the notion that wealth is, as they so frequently say, "like a pie."

The rich therefore "take the largest slice," which leaves guests, customers, and workers with "almost nothing," and the pie "dwindles and shrinks" until there is nothing left.

In the real world, though, where most people outside of academia dwell, freedom makes "the pie" continually bigger.

Do you know why?

Because wealth is *produced*. It is created. It is not some static thing for which people scavenge. Wealth is made. Wealth changes with new technologies. Which is why whale oil is no longer used, nor candles, nor kerosine, nor wood stoves, nor coal stoves, and so on.

Wealth begets wealth.

As energy begets energy, so wealth begets wealth — and for precisely the same reasons.

Because of the limitless ingenuity of the human mind when it's left free, wealth and the creation of wealth is limitless and continual.

Voluntary exchanges are *always* "positive-sum," or they wouldn't be voluntary.

Neither do profit and competition nullify collaboration nor any sort of goodwill among humans.

Socialists pit profit and competition against an ideal of sharing and collaboration. But rather than being a wicked, stolen good, profit is a crucial incentive for collaborative human action.

People are always searching for the best and cheapest products in order to satisfy their needs, and their demands raise prices. The prospect of profit quickly pushes entrepreneurs into producing what people want—and what they are willing to pay for. Profits illustrate how much people value an entrepreneur's services. Consumers only pay if the entrepreneur satisfies their desires.

As long as there are profits to be made, others enter the market. The competition spurs entrepreneurs to make production more efficient and cheaper, because the greater the competition, the more the businessman will have to do to earn the customer's business. As more goods enter the market, consumers can be more picky about whom to purchase from, and prices drop. It's their own demand that sets the prices, and once they are satisfied and there's not as much profit in the business, entrepreneurs shift to making other things that people want.

(Ibid)

Free-exchange is often described by laissez-faire economists as a "voting system" — a voting system of what needs to be produced. Every single cent that is spent acts as a vote for how best to use resources that must be created and developed. Profits direct entrepreneurs toward what people want most urgently. The resulting production is a form of collaboration rather than exploitation. People can do more, because they don't have to do everything themselves, and they can focus on what they do best. This process is also called specialization, which is also known as the division of labor.

The progressive left commits an egregious error when it says, as it so often does — and without so much as a *cursory* glance at the hard statistical data — that "only the rich have gotten richer."

The error is amplified when they then proceed to lambast laissez-faire, which, incidentally, has never existed in full, and certainly not for the last two-hundred years.

Free and voluntary exchange has made *everyone*

wealthier — by light years — and nothing else in the history of the world has come remotely close to matching it. But more than that: free and voluntary exchange has made everyone wealthier *not* only in terms of income but also in terms of the overall quality of life, and in terms of the things people own, the technology to which people have access, so that today, in America, for example, over eighty percent of people officially *below* the poverty line nonetheless own televisions, computers, smart phones, and more, and have ready access to clean running water, food, and medicine.

There is a very specific reason there's never been a famine in the United States, and it is the same reason that people don't die of starvation in the United States, as they do in, for instance, much of India and Africa and North Korea. If that fact *alone* doesn't tell you something significant about freedom and voluntary exchange — no matter where on the bullshit political spectrum you place yourself — you, I submit, are ignoring a staggering amount of factual data.

Studies show, furthermore, that "most people born to the richest fifth of Americans fall out of that bracket within twenty years," while most of those born to the poorest fifth climb to a higher quintile and even to the top.

As Hayek and von Mises both, in absolutely no uncertain terms, showed:

"The businessman [and businesswoman] owe their wealth to his customers, and this wealth is inevitably lost or diminished when others enter the market who can better satisfy the consumer through lower prices and/or a better quality of goods and services."

Elaborating on this insight, the previously mentioned economist Antonis Giannakopoulos, who is, like me, an admirer of the Austrian school of economics, writes this:

The problem with income inequality today is that it *isn't* entirely a byproduct of the free market but instead is the result of a market crippled by interventionist policies, such as regulations, expensive licenses, and the most complicated tax system in the history of this country [America]. Such restrictions have limited competition and made wealth creation more difficult, causing the stagnation of the middle and lower classes.

Though leftists contend that these restrictions protect people from the "dangers" of the free market, they actually protect the corporate interests that progressives claim to stand against.

Colossal businesses like Amazon and Walmart in fact *favor* higher minimum wages and increased regulations. They have the funds to implement them with ease, and such regulations end up acting as a protective barrier, keeping startups and potential competitors from entering the market. With competition blocked, these businesses can grow artificially large and don't have to work as hard to earn people's business. Instead they can spend money on lawyers and DC lobbyists to fence small businesses out of the market.

Ironically, efforts to regulate businesses in the name of protecting laborers and consumers harms small businesses and makes everyone less equal than they could be in a free market.

(Ibid)

Freedom is not the problem. *Regulation* is.

Humans must fight error by unmasking false doctrines and expounding truth.

The truth is that thing which corresponds accurately to reality. Truth and accuracy are in this sense synonymous.

The fundamental social phenomena is the division of labor, which includes corollarily freedom of exchange and human cooperation. The only alternative to this is some form of governmental coercion and state-sanctioned compulsion and force.

The entire premise of redistributive equality and egalitarianism – that equal is the total good and the total goal – must be rejected.

How do you help the poor? You allow people the freedom to voluntarily act charitably, which people will.

How do I know?

Because that's exactly what they did in America

— before government crushed private charity and made it compulsory.

Because when people are left free, the energy and enthusiasm and goodwill — as well as the wealth — all of which are the natural outgrowth of freedom, pours forth.

EGALITARIAN HORROR STORY

"It was toward the middle of the twentieth century that the inhabitants of many European countries came, in general unpleasantly, to the realization that their fate could be influenced directly by intricate and abstruse books of philosophy. Their bread, their work, their private lives began to depend on this or that decision in disputes on principles to which, until then, they had never paid any attention. In their eyes, the philosopher had always been a sort of dreamer whose divagations had no effect on reality. The average human being, even if he had once been exposed to it, wrote philosophy off as utterly impractical and useless. Therefore the great intellectual work of the Marxists could easily pass as just one more variation on a sterile pastime. Only a few

189

individuals understood the causes and probable consequences of this general indifference."

— *The Captive Mind*, Czeslaw Milosz (winner of the Nobel Prize for Literature, 1980)

THE POWER of ideas can be seen no more starkly than in the fact that people subscribe to them without any hesitation, wavering, or scruples.

As captured so perfectly in the Czeslaw Milosz passage quoted at the top of this chapter, societies and any concrete order of social affairs are the *direct* outcome of ideas.

Ideas come from thinking, which by its very nature is an individualized act.

Ideas have consequences, both for good and for ill, and the determining factor is the truth or falsehood of the ideas being propounded.

The following is a real-life illustration — writ sickeningly large — of what can happen when false ideas grip a society. In this case, it is the false idea that individuals do not exist but are merely parts of a collective. This is what can result when the idea of individuality, individualism, and independent thinking are not regarded as primary but replaced instead with the ideology of egalitarianism by force:

"When the Khmer Rouge seized power in April 1975, they did so with the intention of obliterating its hierarchical political culture in order to reconstruct Cambodian society from ground zero as the world's most egalitarian, and therefore revolutionary social order."

That passage comes from historian Karl Jackson, in a heartbreaking book, published by Princeton Press, called *Cambodia 1975 – 1978*. In this book, Jackson describes the Khmer Rouge (which was the name of the socialist-communist-Marxist party that took over Cambodia in the mid-1970's) as "sectarians and radical egalitarians [who] saw the diversity and differences between people as the root of all evil."

This ideology was extrapolated directly from the ideas of Karl Marx and Friedrich Engels.

The Khmer Rouge was led by a cult-of-personality named Pol Pot, Western educated, who was also the architect of the Killing Fields – a seemingly incomprehensible genocide where Cambodian cities were systematically depopulated, and the entire Cambodian citizenry was enslaved on collective farms with a horrifyingly draconian ideology-of-equality imposed upon all.

"Typically, the slightest dissent would be punished by the offender getting clubbed or starved to death, and so many Cambodians were dispatched by such methods (approximately 1.7 million between 1975 and 1979 according to one estimate) that fields filled with corpses became the macabre hallmark of the regime" (Ibid).

From the *Journal of Asian Studies* (1998):

"First, they tried to eliminate the use of linguistic registers that connoted kinship, age and other social differences. The word comrade, *mitt*, was suppose to replace titles, honorifics and even kin terms. Second, many non-verbal cues that connoted status, such as polite greeting forms and bending down before superiors, were also discouraged."

A historian by the name of Jay Jordens writes that the "Khmer Rouge realized Buddhism was at the core of Khmer ideas of social hierarchy. Thus by abolishing religion and destroying all vestiges of Buddhism; monks, texts, images, rituals, and so on, they might destroy the moral underpinnings of the beliefs in 'unequal souls'" (*Propaganda, Politics and Violence in Cambodia*, 1996).

And from the website Asia Pacific Curriculum:

By 1977, the distrust on the part of the leadership had reached paranoiac heights and the purges of suspected traitors increased. Even the ranks of the Khmer Rouge cadres themselves were purged, sending increasingly larger numbers of them and their families to prisons where they were tortured and then murdered. The most notorious of these prisons was S-21, a high school in Phnom Penh that was converted into a prison and torture centre run by Kaing Guek Eav, also known as Duch. Out of an estimated 15,000 prisoners who were sent to S-21, only seven survived.

Prisoners housed there were photographed and tortured to produce confessions. When the interrogators were finished, the prisoners' corpses were carried by truck to the "killing fields" outside of Phnom Penh. There are approximately 20,000 of these mass graves in various locationsin the country.

The relatively short time that Pol Pot ruled — approximately four years — was a living nightmare. An estimated *one-quarter* of the Cambodian population was killed. I ask you to please pause for a moment and process that.

These were each individual human beings, like you and me, with individual human lives and loves and passions and dreams and problems and sadnesses and joys, and their individual lives were real and important. Yet they were murdered as though they were nothing — nothing but cogs in a collectivist machine which in reality existed only inside the warped and grotesque mind of a dictator.

The Cambodian people who survived survived only on "a ladle of watery rice gruel a day." They were forced into back-breaking labor most of their waking hours – separated from their families, and do you know the specific reason for this?

The answer is that families don't matter much in

the Communist ideology, since all humans are equal comrades: your parents and siblings and children the same to you as parents, siblings, and children of all other people, even if you've never seen any of these people in your life, nor they you.

Pol Pot's regime forced the Cambodian people to eat in spectacularly unsanitary cooperatives, treating them worse than the poorly treated farm animals. They lived under incessant terror of being reported, even for minor acts "such as taking a coconut from a tree or allowing cattle to graze in the wrong field."

An incalculable number of people died as a direct result of these filthy, terror-stricken conditions.

Vietnamese minority groups in particular were singled out for persecution and annihilation. So were the Cham Muslim minorities.

Survivors report that urbanites suffered harder work and even greater suspicion than the peasantry.

Virtually the entire population labored on farms, and do you know why? Because the ideology of egalitarianism decrees that all humans do everything the same. Thus, since the government could neither force people into instant expertise and specialization, which takes time and study and practice, nor the comparatively luxurious standards of urban living, which must come from a level of wealth and production they could not come close to affording, the government went for the opposite: slaughtering intellectuals and evacuating the cities overnight and forcing everyone, no matter their knowledge and training, into impoverished subsistence agriculture — abolishing, with astonishing speed and extreme force, all specialization and the division of labor, which is, of course, hierarchical and therefore regarded by all egalitarian standards as "undesirable."

In terms of the sheer numbers of individual lives taken, Hitler, Mao, and Stalin killed far more people than Pol Pot, and yet Pol Pot and his genocidal regime stands out among them all — for being, in my opinion, the most horrific and evil-perfect-practitioner of this ideology: an ideology that regards individuality as non-existent, people only worth anything to the extent that they help produce food "collectively." Thus the Khmer Rouge slogans, written and posted where the Cambodian people could read them, contained a sick and shocking disregard for individual human life:

"To keep you is no benefit. To destroy you is no loss. Better to kill an innocent by mistake than spare an enemy by mistake."

The Khmer Rouge is among the most ghastly of proofs about which you will ever read regarding the paramount role of ideas in human life.

For the people who harangue, harass, and ridicule those among us defending individualism, individuality, and individual rights, who think that the idea of egalitarian-socialism is nothing to remotely consider or entertain, please read deeply about Pol Pot and the Khemer Rouge — the obliteration of individual rights, the destruction of the entire concept of individuality and independent thinking: read what it led to in Cambodia, and then come back and harangue. There's plenty more to say — beginning with the fact that egalitarianism is still, right up to this present moment, in one form or another, *the* defining characteristic and cornerstone of virtually all leftist ideology going back the last two-hundred years. It's most recent iteration is the "privilege-inequality" narrative, which has infected the world like a plague.

As Vincent Cook expressed it so well:

Mass death is certainly no stranger to Communism. Even today a terrible famine stalks North Korea to remind us of the lethal nature of Marxism. However, Pol Pot has earned a special place in the history of Marxian Communism as his Khmer Rouge earned the special distinction of being the one Communist movement in history to actually attempt the full and consistent implementation of the ideals of Karl Marx.

Most Marxists would recoil at the suggestion that Pol Pot is the logical conclusion of their social philosophy, yet any honest assessment of Marx's theory cannot conceal the fact that the radical egalitarianism of the Khmer Rouge is precisely what Marx predicted would be the ultimate culmination of all human history. It must be clearly kept in mind that industrial socialism, as it was known in the former Soviet Union and other mainstream Marxist states, is not the endpoint of Marx's philosophy of history. In his view, the abolition of capitalist production relations is only the first stage of the worldwide proletarian revolution.

Marx anticipated that there would be a radical redistribution of wealth and a withering of the global socialist state (the "crude" stage of communism) followed by a fundamental transformation of human nature as all individual culture, personality, and economic uniqueness disappeared (the "higher" stage of communism). Marx looked forward to a time when individuals would be freed from an alleged alienation from their own humanity supposedly caused by the division of labor and money-based economic transactions. Individuality would be replaced by a new generic "species-being" [Marx's term] personality, a personality that would specialize in nothing and be an expert at everything.

It is now a fact fairly well-known, even among socialists, that economic calculation under pure socialism is an impossibility. And yet compared with the idea that any country or economy could survive, let alone prosper, after government abolishes the division of labor — simultaneously crushing all individuality in the process — the calculation problem seems downright minor, even though in reality it is not minor at all: yet it *seems* so simply because this latter idea is such sheer madness.

"Most Communist movements, faced with the utter infeasibility of industrial production under socialist central planning (let alone an abolition of the division of labor), chose to reconcile themselves with capitalism in various ways and to defer the Marxist ideal of higher Communism to a remote future that would conveniently never come. Some Communists, notably the Soviets and especially the Yugoslavs, practically admitted that the species-being ideal would never be realized and were willing to settle for varying degrees of centralized socialistic control mixed with elements of capitalism" (ibid).

Maoists, however, remained pure — at least for a time.

Thus the "Cultural Revolution" of China which vainly tried to transform human nature itself — individuals do not exist, these Maoists also preached — until, that is, its stupendous failure forced even the most radical of Maoists to step back and reevaluate. This failure-followed-by-reevaluation changed Maoism across Asia and the world — with one appalling exception: Pol Pot and the Khmer Rouge.

Pol Pot understood that industrialization and the

cities which emerge through the division of labor would have to be eliminated if the Khmer Rouge were to come anywhere close to an egalitarian society. This is why almost immediately after the Khmer Rouge took power (in April of 1975), the regime began evacuating Phnom Penh. They were, in a very real and literal sense, merely acting with the courage of their Communist convictions.

"The worst that can be said of Pol Pot was that he was sincere," Vincent Cook correctly wrote, and continued:

> The Cambodian people were in fact freed of the "alienation" of a division of labor and individual personality, and were reduced to a perfectly uniform egalitarian existence on the collective farms. If the cruel reality of the Khmer Rouge slave state didn't quite come up to the extravagant eschatological expectations of Marxist true-believers, the fault lies exclusively with those who think of the Marxist pattern of historical development and its egalitarian outcome as a desirable state of affairs. It is not enough to say of Pol Pot, as Prince Sihanouk did: 'Let him be dead. Now our nation will be very peaceful.' We must also acknowledge that a Pol Pot-type passion for equality remains as a threat to the peace and well-being of every nation even if the former dictator himself is dead.

There should be no forgetting the crimes of the Khmer Rouge — no matter how much time has passed or will pass — no whitewashing them, no cultural amnesia concerning them, nor any diminishment whatsoever nor rationalization of their utter evil, especially not by academic elites, like Noam Chomsky and Howard Zinn and all the others who once praised Pol Pot for his Communist convictions and the "just society" he despotically built. Nor should these atrocities be whitewashed and forgotten by any of the ideologically bankrupt intellectuals explicitly calling for Communism today and telling us, as a "reminder," that "Communism is good."

These people must be ideologically confronted and exposed and defeated — routed — on the battleground of ideas, because the truth is that when the facts are made clear and their philosophies presented in full, without their interminable equivocations, circumlocutions, obfuscations, and jargon, there is no argument — they don't have one — and so they don't stand a chance. And do you know why they don't have an argument?

Because nobody has a right to the life or labor of any other individual human being.

If anyone ever tells you differently, ask them this: How?

Ask them from where their edicts and premises derive.

Ask them by what natural order of affairs — what fact within nature, either human nature or nature apart from humans — do they derive such a doctrine. Because in the history of the entire world, no good answer has ever been given to this question, and do you know why?

Because no good answer for it exists.

The Cambodian Killing Fields should stand eternally as a horrific, monolithic, twisted moment to the philosophy of egalitarianism, and the human race should never forget that any minister of force preaching the egalitarian doctrine-of-envy — which is to say, anti-individualism — that person, that minister of force, is an ideological offspring and disciple of Pol Pot.

I am well aware that most people today espousing socialism and egalitarianism — especially those who've grown up in the first-world and take its comparative freedom for granted — are not despots-in-waiting, tyrants-to-be, or full-blown dictators of the blackest breed. But I know also that Stalin, Mao, Pol Pot, et al, are exactly where and to what these politico-ethical-economic ideologies lead.

I know also that once a principle has been breeched, even to a small degree, it becomes increasingly easy — easy and then easier and easier — for that principle to be breeched again and again. So that you soon hear people saying: "What do you mean, government can't *legitimately* restrict an individual's freedom of action, or expropriate her property? Certainly it can. Governments do it all the time, as they've been doing it for decades. Look at military conscription — the draft — or look at 1913, when the Federal Reserve was created and then, that same year, laws came into being which passed the national income tax, which is certainly a type of expropriation, and then Herbert Hoover and his passage of Smoot–Hawley, which paved the way for the New Deal, with all its price and wage controls, and then Social Security, which was meant to be temporary, and then Medicare and Medicaid and then TARP, followed by Barack Obama's trillion-dollar 'stimulus,' whose thousands of pages nobody read in full before it was rammed through and made into the law of the land, and then his taxpayer-funded bailouts and his taxpayer subsidizations of 'renewables' and then Obamacare. Why should Donald Trump's new laws be any different?"

Why, indeed?

Thus are new laws endlessly enacted, and endlessly justified. And then one day, freedom is gone, and nobody quite knows how. Or cares.

POSTMODERNISM: THE DESTRUCTION OF THOUGHT

"It's our word. Don't use it. Don't try to define it. Above all don't label us with it. Even if we apply it to ourselves."

THE ONLY MEANS by which knowledge and human progress can ultimately be sabotaged is through the systematic rejection of inductive reasoning, which forms the underpinnings not just of all science and the scientific-method, but of the entirety of human apprehension.

No scientist— whether researcher or practitioner or both, whether biologist, chemist, physicist, geologist, climate scientist, or any other — could pursue actual knowledge without first having some idea of what knowledge is and how to gain and attain it.

All scientists, therefore, whether they know it explicitly or not, need some sort of theory of knowledge.

This theory, in turn, grows from the most fundamental science: the science of philosophy.

The science of knowledge belongs specifically to that branch of philosophy called epistemology.

Epistemology — from the Greek word *episteme,* which means "knowledge" — is an extraordinarily complicated discipline that begins with three simple words: consciousness is awareness.

All scientists, I repeat, need a theory of knowledge, and this theory of knowledge subsequently affects every aspect of a scientist's approach to her research — from the questions she asks, to the answers she finds, to the hypothesis and theories then developed and later built-upon.

Very rare geniuses like Galileo and Newton and perhaps even Kepler (who, for all his mathematical brilliance and tireless work, held to a metaphysical viewpoint deeply flawed) were ferociously innovative in epistemology as well as physics specifically, in systematizing and codifying the core principles of the inductive-method, which they all three came to through their scrupulous use of scientific experiment.

Experiment *is* induction.

Benjamin Franklin flying a kite into a lightning storm in order to test a notion (i.e. theory and idea) he had about electricity, with a metal key tied to the kite string, is an example of the inductive method at work.

Induction more than anything else — including deduction — is the method of reason and the engine of human knowledge and therefore progress.

A proper epistemology teaches a scientist, as it teaches everyone else concerned with comprehension and actual learning, how to exercise the full power of the human mind — which is to say, how to reach the broadest abstractions while not losing sight of the specifics or, it you prefer, the concretes.

A proper epistemolgy teaches how to synthesize sensory data into a step-by-step pyramid of knowledge, culminating in the grasp of fundamental truths whose context applies to the whole universe. Galileo's laws of motion and Newton's laws of optics, as well as his laws of gravity, are examples of this. If humans transport to a sector of the universe where these laws do not hold true, it still *doesn't* invalidate them here. The context here remains.

The significance of this principle cannot be exaggerated or overstated.

In this way, knowledge expands as context expands.

The fact that all truths are *by definition* contextual does not invalidate absolute truth and knowledge thereby, but just the opposite: context is the means by which we measure and validate absolute truth.

Epistemologically, postmodernism is the rejection of this entire process.

Postmodernism, in all its vicious variations, is a term devoid of any real content, and for this reason dictionaries and philosophy dictionaries offer very little help in defining it.

And yet postmodernism has today become almost universally embraced as *the* dominant philosophy of science — which is the primary reason that science crumbles before our eyes under its corrupt and carious epistemology.

Postmodernism, like everything else, is a philosophical issue. Accordingly, postmodernism's tentacles have extended into every major branch of philosophy — from metaphysics, to epistemology, to esthetics, to ethics, to politics, to economics.

In order to get any kind of grasp on postmodernism, one must grasp first that postmodernism doesn't want to be defined. Its distinguishing characteristic is in the dispensing of all definitions — because definitions presuppose a firm and comprehensible universe. Accurate definitions are guardians of the human mind against the chaos of psychological disintegration.

You must understand next that postmodernism is a revolt against the philosophical movement that immediately preceded it: Modernism.

We're told by postmodernists today that modernism and everything that modernism stands for is dead.

Thus, whereas modernism preached the existence of independent reality, postmodernism preaches anti-realism, solipsism, and "reality" as a term that always requires quotation marks.

Whereas modernism preached reason and science, postmodernism preaches social subjectivism and knowledge by consensus.

Whereas modernism preached free-will and self-governance, postmodernism preaches determinism and the rule of the collective.

Whereas modernism preached the freedom of each and every individual, postmodernism preaches multiculturalism, environmentalism, egalitarianism by coercion, social-justice.

Whereas modernism preached free-markets and free-exchange, postmodernism preaches Marxism and its little bitch: statism.

Whereas modernism preached objective meaning and knowledge, postmodernism preaches deconstruction and no-knowledge — or, if there is any meaning at all (and there's not), it's subjective and ultimately unverifiable.

In the words of one of postmodernism's high priests, Michel Foucault: "It is meaningless to speak in the name of — or against — Reason, Truth, or Knowledge."

Why?

Because according to Mr. Foucault again: "Reason is the ultimate language of madness."

We can thus define postmodernism as follows:

It is the philosophy of absolute agnosticism — agnosticism in the literal sense of the word — meaning: a philosophy that preaches the impossibility of human knowledge.

What this translates to in day-to-day life is pure subjectivism without any real standards, ethical or otherwise, and the ramifications of which are, in the area of literature, for example, no meaning, completely open interpretation, unintelligibility.

Othello, therefore, is as much about racism and affirmative-action as it is about jealousy.

Since there is no objective meaning in art, all interpretations are equally valid.

Postmodernism is anti-reason, anti-logic, anti-intelligibility.

Politically, it is anti-freedom. It explicitly advocates leftist, collectivist Neo-Marxism and the deconstruction of industry, as well as the dispensing of inalienable rights to property and person.

There is, however, a profound and fatal flaw built into the very premise of postmodernism, which flaw makes postmodernism impossible to take seriously and simple to reject:

If reason and logic are invalid and no objective knowledge is possible, then the whole pseudo-philosophy of postmodernism is also invalidated.

One can't use proof, reason, or the reasoning process, even in a flawed form, to try and prove that reason is false.

HARD ROCK MINER

THE HARD ROCK miner died last night, a thin man, a strong man, with the soft-sad eyes of a thoughtful child.

His name was Neil. He'd been a miner most of his life. He chewed Copenhagen and played guitar (he loved hard rock). In Vietnam he'd been awarded the Silver Star for an act of great courage.

After the war, at twenty-five, he went to work in a uranium mine outside Moab called The Gentleman Sloan. Two years later, he moved into the coal-mining country of east-central Wyoming. Then, at age thirty-one, he drove into the spiky mountains of southwestern Colorado and began working in a gold mine called The Equity, and this is where he remained for the rest of his life.

His end began suddenly, less than ten months ago, when he was fifty-eight-years-years-old. He found one unforgettable evening, a terrifying eruption of crystal-like growths all along his ribcage. His doctors punched cylindrical core samples out his skin. They drilled him full of holes and loaded him with tubes like tiny sticks of dynamite, blasting caps of pinkish-blue. Cancer is what they found. Cancer blooming like clusters of quartz everywhere beneath his skin.

The strangeness of it was not lost on him: that something so small could take down a man his size —a man so living and vital, a man, in short, like him.

He had not expected to die this way. He thought his end would come in the cold dark caves among the echo-drip of black water, or from blacklung.

Or perhaps on his way home from work one star-sprent frozen night, a wall of white would come pounding down out of the galactic blackness above, building in a moment a skyscraper of snow atop him and his jeep. But it had not been so.

Enraged, he cursed at first. And overnight his skin went totally slack, the flesh about the bones—a padding—melting like candlewax. His temples grew indrawn, clustered with silver veins. For reasons the doctors could not explain, the cave of his mouth began to morph so that his palate became a ceiling of ribbed rock, tasting of sulfur and sprouting minia-ture stalactites of limey tissue, or bone. The gold-and-copper of his hair, which had lasted him his whole life, now faded to galena threads, threads of winking lead.

Over the years, the mines had exacted heavy tolls upon his health, as mines so often will. A chronic cough plagued him the last decade of his life. He had poor blood circulation, his veins dying like underground streams inside his skin, and his skin, from head-to-toe, transparent, mica-thin.

Twenty years previous, on a cold autumn morning, while he was exploring an abandoned shaft, he was brought up short by an iron fist clenching inside his chest. It sent him running back in the direction he had come. He'd barely made it. Lack of oxygen, they said, had caused a small heart attack. Thereafter his "ticker" (as he termed it) was never again the same.

And who could forget the time, early on in his mining career, when a stone slab the size of a boxcar busted loose from the low rock ceiling above and mashed him face-first into the soggy ground. He lay like that for two days and two nights, unable to move at all, while his headlamp subsided into ultimate black, and he, half-delirious, heard the whole time the purling of underground streams rocking gently by. This, he thought, is it: this is how I die.

His rescuers told him later that the softness of the earth and the freezing cold had, in part, saved him, but mainly, they whispered among themselves, it was the sheer strength of his will, and the strength of his muscle and bone.

Still, for all this, he loved his work. He loved the whole lifestyle, loved it with his body and soul. He loved the sound of sluicing water, the smell of wet mineral and adamantine stone. He loved the vitreous air where he worked (and worked), the air itself exuding sparseness, the reek of ozone and pine. He loved the sandy tailing ponds, their poisonous waters, the sound of the ravens grokking at him from the firs all around the mine, and the firs themselves stunted and dark and weird, crepitating with human-like moans. He loved all the magpie and the chipmunks and the fat brown marmots – "whistle pigs," he called them – sunning themselves in the sharp western sunlight the short summers long. He loved the arsenic-burned rocks they scorched their bellies on.

He loved the massive gray shadows that tilted the ground, and the white dusty earth that the ubiquitous mountains cast their shadows upon.

He loved Sugarloaf peak in spring, with its necktie of mist and wig of snow, and the ragged mountains beyond poking the sky – and that sky forever, in his memory, tarnished like zinc, or a verdigris stone.

The rarified air he could never get enough of: the glassy gales in autumn and the mean winter wind pouring down from the milky sky above, rushing through the conifers in sporadic bursts and blowing the black cliffs bare of vapor and snow, showing naked chines of rock – rock everywhere, the smell of rock, rock rearing up into the high-altitude air, angular walls all along the roads that led up to the mines.

To him this was worth ten years of life.

And his life was not yours, or mine.

Our final meeting came on my last day of work, before I moved out of the San Juans for good. He was just coming on shift, swing. He stood at the entrance of the shaft, half turned away. A long shadow from the mouth of the cave fell diagonally across him, and in his hardhat and yellow slicker, the hard rock miner looked like one about ready to fight fires, or cyclones. His headlamp was not turned on yet. His boots were covered in year-old muck. His gloves poked partially out his bib. For some reason, then, I do not know why, he turned to me and waved goodbye. Then he swiveled back around and lumbered alone into the black dripping shaft, where no light shone at all, and then he disappeared forever from my site, underground.

WAITRESS

SHE WORKS in a diner called the Desert Rose, which sits along the northwestern edge of Colorado, near the Utah border. The diner is a small and undistinguished affair, all dark wood and oxblood-leather, worn and weathered, but always brightly lit and burning like a little beacon in a high American wasteland. Triangles of cherry pie sit bleeding in the pie case, and strips of honey-yellow flypaper spiral from the low stucco ceiling.

She was born and raised in a tiny mountain town one-hundred miles southeast. She grew up slender and pretty, a kind of patrician's elegance about her, self-reliant, drinking beer and smoking cigarettes with all the other small-town boys and girls: one of them, yet always somehow slightly apart without meaning to be. She began working when she was in the tenth grade — an indefatigable worker, no matter the job — and she's not stopped working since. Waiting tables is what she's done for most of her life. She graduated high school but never went to college. After that, she drifted awhile, developed a taste for books, black coffee, functional knowledge.

By age thirty-seven, she'd already buried two husbands, both miners, one killed in a car crash, the other dead by disease. She has two teenage children who love her. Now, unmarried, no longer young but not yet old, she is beautiful still, and elegant. She listens to soft jazz on her transistor radio and reads and reads in her rented apartment that's too small for three.

There have been many other jobs — night-auditor, bank-teller, housecleaner — but waitressing is the one she's always come back to. There are no special skills in her repertoire, no trade beyond waitressing. She's well-read, her mind of a naturally speculative cast, and she quotes to herself from old poets ("full many a flower is born to blush unseen and waste its sweetness on the desert air").

At twilight, invariably, there's a sense of melancholy that comes over her.

Fifty feet behind the diner called Desert Rose, a cluster of cottonwoods grows along the banks of a sea-green river. They are ancient and massive trees. Wind moves sluggishly through their dusty boughs, and moonlike globes of cotton orbit the bodies of the trees and fall soundlessly into the molecular water. Sparse grass grows along the desert floor, and the desert stretches off into the wooly horizon.

At the end of her shift, she likes to stand at the back porch of the diner and listen to the wind sifting through the grass. Certain times of the year there are blue and violet flowers, slender and strange, which grow among the river stalks. Sometimes she thinks she can smell their sweetness on the desert air. The bone-colored moon rises meanwhile in the east and fills a small quadrant of the sky, suffusing the clouds with its soft and sulfurous light.

WHISKEY WISDOM

THE TINIEST WAYS YOU TOUCH
SOMEONE'S LIFE ADD UP; THEY
ACCUMULATE. IF YOU SHOW
SOMEONE ENOUGH LAUGHTER
AND LIGHT AND KINDNESS,
THIS PERSON WILL ~~LIKELY~~
RESPOND LIKEWISE.

THE SUDSBUSTER

HE WAS one of the mellow, the soft-spoken, the sandy-haired — one who preferred to be alone.

His name was Mark, a dishwasher at age forty-five.

He was a dreamer, a wanderer, and he valued his freedom above all. Dishwashing jobs he could always find.

Our paths crossed and re-crossed at the Café Claire, where I was tending bar. The Café Claire stood on the outskirts of an industrial town, near the railroad tracks and near his temporary home. Sometimes he'd sit at the end of the bar, before his shift or after, and drink black coffee. Sometimes he'd speak to me, and sometimes he would not.

He was a tidy man, and orderly. He organized things in an oddly geometrical way. He did not drink, he did not smoke, he did not use drugs. He was clean-living and in good shape, neither depressed nor its opposite.

He was single, without children.

And he was free.

He read a lot — fiction, non-fiction, poetry, prose — to help endure, perhaps, the knives of lust that can so frequently strike. He had the quietude of one who has gone a long time without sex.

His home was an efficiency apartment — a "hutch," he called it — with good plumbing. (This mattered to him.) He dealt only in cash and he was good with his money. He saved, he moved on. Sometimes he worked on farms, sometimes he loaded and unloaded freight, sometimes he carried hod. But when I first met him and asked him what he did, he said "I'm a sudsbuster."

So in the way of things, he would come behind my bar at times, when I was busy, and, without asking me and without being asked by anyone, he'd wash my dishes. I loved him for that. He was fast on his feet and knew how to work around people, so that nobody was in anybody's way. Buried in Bloody Marys and martinis, I'd glance over and see him plunged to his elbows in suds, his gold-rim spectacles, which somehow endeared him to me, filled with the burning bar light, his neat goatee damp with perspiration and pied with skeins of gray. Working with somebody in this way creates a deep and ineradicable bond.

Two or three times, I saw him outside work while I was in my car. Each time, he was walking alone along the railroad tracks, at dusk like some solitary figure carved from the coming dark. This was a grizzled landscape, a prairie desert of Euclidian perfection, full of rings and radii, vast yet traversed only by a single road: an isolate highway humming day or night with Mack truck tires. The wind ferried tumbleweeds across the lion's pelt land. Deadwood everywhere stood silvery-gray, like the moon above, and invariably whenever I saw him walking, a feeling of melancholy came over me, a melancholy for him, I am not sure why.

This, though, is not about pity or pathos, and Mark was not a person to pitied. This, rather, is about one man out of many millions making his way in the land of the free: the USA.

OTHER BOOKS

Reservation Trash: **the remarkable story of a Navajo runner**

Made in the USA
Coppell, TX
22 November 2020

41902120R00142